Modern Library Chronicles

INVENTING JAPAN

IAN BURUMA

INVENTING JAPAN

1853–1964

A MODERN LIBRARY CHRONICLES BOOK

THE MODERN LIBRARY

NEW YORK

2003 Modern Library Edition

Published in Great Britain by Weidenfeld & Nicolson,
a division of Orion Publishing Group Ltd.

LIBRARY OF CONGRESS CATALOGING-IN-PUBLICATION DATA
Buruma, Ian.
Inventing Japan, 1853–1964 / Ian Buruma.
p.   cm. — (Modern Library chronicles ; 11)
"A Modern Library chronicles book."
Includes bibliographical references and index.
ISBN 0-679-64085-1 (hc. : alk paper)
1. Japan—History—1868–   2. Japan—History—Restoration,
1853–1870.   I. Title.   II. Series.
DS881.9 .B87   2003
952.03—dc21
2002026346

Modern Library website address: www. modernlibrary.com
Printed in the United States of America on acid-free paper
2 4 6 8 9 7 5 3 1

CONTENTS

INVENTING JAPAN

PROLOGUE: THE TOKYO OLYMPICS

In 1964, Japan rejoined the world. The postwar period of poverty, humiliation, and, until 1952, Allied occupation was finally over, and the boom years of the economic miracle had begun. In a formal, political sense, Japan had already rejoined the world as a sovereign nation in September 1951, when Prime Minister Yoshida Shigeru signed the San Francisco Peace Treaty with his country's former enemies, though not yet with China or the Soviet Union. But the autumn of 1964, when the Olympics came to Tokyo, was to be the great ceremonial celebration of Japan's peaceful, postwar democratic revival. No longer a defeated nation in disgrace, Japan was respectable now. After years of feverish construction, of highways and stadiums, hotels, sewers, overhead railways, and subway lines, Tokyo was ready to receive the world with a grand display of love, peace, and sports.

To anyone sitting in Tange Kenzo's grand new stadium on the afternoon of October 10, seeing the athletes from ninety-four nations marching by, Americans in cowboy hats and Japanese in red blazers, with Emperor Hirohito offering a friendly wave to the world from his royal box and eight thousand white doves of peace fluttering toward the bright blue sky, it must have seemed an awfully long time ago that Japan walked out of the League of Nations in 1933 and joined the Axis powers in 1940, hoping to divide the world with Hitler and Mussolini. Manchuria, Nanking, Pearl Harbor, Bataan, Okinawa, and Manila—all that appeared to be forgotten now, as millions of Japanese expressed their joyful feelings in little poems published in the papers every day. One good citizen expressed his emotions like this:

> One and then another, ninety-four flags.
> Some, perhaps, have met on battlefields.

The poem is less notable for its literary quality than for the odd use of the word *perhaps*. But as Edward Seidensticker, from whose book I quote, put it, this might be taken "as a mark of the Japanese tendency to soften things a bit."

By 1964, the chief Japanese symbol of wartime suffering, and subsequently of Japanese pacifism, was the bombing of Hiroshima. As a reminder of Japan's peaceful intentions, and perhaps also, in a fit of self-pity, of Japan's own suffering in the past, the young man chosen to light the Olympic flame was born in Hiroshima on the day it was obliterated by the A-bomb. As the flame was lit, fighter jets of the Japanese Self-Defense Forces scrambled over Tokyo with the entirely pacific intent of drawing the five Olympic rings in the sky.

The Japanese impressed the world with their friendly manners and efficient organization. Nothing was allowed to go wrong. And they managed to win plenty of medals, too: sixteen gold, a tally bettered only by the United States and the Soviet Union. Japanese took their sporting records seriously, perhaps more so than was entirely necessary. Two Japanese athletes who failed to come up to popular expectations, a marathon runner named Tsubuya Kokichi and a woman hurdler named Yoda Ikuko, later committed suicide. Poor Tsubuya had the peculiarly humiliating experience of entering the stadium in second place, only to be passed in sight of a horrified home crowd by an Englishman just before the finish. His bronze medal was no consolation.

To the Japanese, always acutely conscious of their ranking among nations, sporting victories were one way to soothe memories of wartime defeat. Through the 1950s, the successes in the wrestling ring of a bruiser named Riki Dozan had served as a balm for injured Japanese pride. His fights tended to follow a well-rehearsed pattern. Faced by larger opponents, often of Western origin, who fought dirty, Riki would falter in the early rounds. But then, gradually, inspired by visions of Mount Fuji, the Japanese hero would work himself into a righteous rage and finally, despite his inferior size, overcome the big, blond villain.

There were, however, a few problems with Riki Dozan. For one thing, he was of Korean origin, an official secret that deceived many but not all. And professional wrestling, though entertaining, lacked the cachet of more traditional forms of combat, such as sumo, kendo, or judo. Besides, Riki Dozan was no longer around in the Olympic year. He had been stabbed to death the year before, by a gangster in a Tokyo nightclub. It was time for Japanese to show their prowess in a more traditional manner. So the Japanese Olympic Committee exercised its privilege to choose judo as a new Olympic sport.

Besides the fact that Japanese were likely to win medals in their native sport, judo had another advantage: It would demonstrate the power of skill over brawn. Judo was not about size or muscle power, it was about something infinitely more subtle than that, something almost spiritual. To beat an opponent you needed patience, quickness of mind, and great discipline. A small man could beat a much larger one by using his opponent's bulk against him. Unlike wrestling or boxing, judo demanded mental skills that might well be beyond the power of Westerners, who were used to cruder forms of combat. Put another way, judo would show off the superiority of Japanese culture, of the Japanese spirit.

To make their point, the Japanese included an open division as well as the traditional heavy-, middle-, and light-weight divisions. Any challenger could enter, no matter how large or small. The Japanese favorite to win gold in this category was Kaminaga Akio, a skilled champion who was hefty for a Japanese, but not as big as the Dutch champion, Anton Geesink, a six-foot-six-inch, 267-pound giant. But no matter, Kaminaga would surely beat him. And this would be worth at least a hundred Riki Dozan wins against blond lowlifes on the pro wrestling circuit.

The bout was set on October 23, the last day of the games. Seventeen thousand people crowded into the martial arts hall in the center of Tokyo to see Kaminaga put the crown on Japan's Olympic Games. In every Japanese city, town, and village, people gathered around shop windows to follow the event on TV. This was something nobody wanted to miss. Millions came out to support Kaminaga, on whose broad shoulders Japanese pride now rested. There would be no parliamentary business that day. Patriotic bosses made sure their companies had at least one television set on each floor. People sent verses in praise of Kaminaga to the newspapers. The emperor himself would be watching, too.

For ten minutes, the Japanese and the Dutchman were evenly matched. Kaminaga attacked, Geesink fended him off. Both men watched each other's feet, trying to anticipate the next move, as though they were playing a kind of physical chess game. Then, suddenly, Geesink pounced. With surprising quickness for such a big man, he wrestled

Kaminaga to the mat and pinned him down. The Japanese champion thrashed about, trying to get a grip with his hands. His strong calves hit the mat again and again, like a fish struggling for its life. Finally, the referee called time. Geesink had won.

First there was silence, then sobs of grief. The humiliation was almost too much to bear. Once again, Japanese manhood had been put to the test against superior Western force, and once again it was found wanting. But then an extraordinary thing happened. Moments after his victory, Dutch fans tried to rush to the mat to congratulate their hero. Immediately, however, Geesink raised his hand to stop them and turned to Kaminaga to make his formal bow. The Japanese audience rose to applaud this traditional gesture of respect. And they never forgot it. Geesink, the big Dutch victor in Tokyo who had shown the Japanese what skill as well as bulk could achieve, would be treated as a hero in Japan forever after.

Overconfidence, fanaticism, a shrill sense of inferiority, and a sometimes obsessive preoccupation with national status—these have all played their parts in the history of modern Japan, as we shall see. But one quality has stood out to serve Japan better than any other: the grace to make the best of defeat.

THE BLACK SHIPS

When Commodore Matthew ("Old Matt") Calbraith Perry sailed into Edo Bay on July 8, 1853, with four heavily armed ships, on a mission to open up Japanese ports to American ships, he could be forgiven for thinking the Japanese were an ignorant people. Japan had been cut off from most other countries for roughly two hundred years. Japanese rulers, fearful of foreign aggression and worried that Christianity, promoted by European missionaries, would make their subjects unruly, had outlawed the Christian religion, expelled most foreigners and all priests, and forbidden Japanese to go abroad. Anyone bold enough to defy these rules faced execution, usually of a most gruesome kind. Few were so bold. Trade with China and Korea still went on, but since the 1630s, the Western presence in Japan had been limited to a handful of bored Dutch merchants confined to a tiny man-made island off the city of Nagasaki.

It was one of the most extraordinary confrontations in modern history. There was Perry with his four "black ships of evil," thundering an ominous salute at the Japanese coast by firing his cannon. And there were the Japanese, lined up on the shore, armed with swords and old-fashioned muskets. Commodore Perry insisted on dealing only with the highest representatives of the Japanese government, without really knowing who they were. The distinction in his mind between the emperor, a grand but still powerless figure, and the shogun was fuzzy. The emperor, living in Kyoto, the old imperial capital, was the symbol of Japanese cultural continuity. His duties were ceremonial and spiritual, while the shogun ruled, as the samurai generalissimo, from his seat in Edo, today's Tokyo. From 1603, the shoguns all belonged to the Tokugawa clan, hence the name of their government, Tokugawa *bakufu* (shogunate), also known as Edo *bakufu*.

Perry, however, unaware of all this, kept on insisting that his letter from President Millard Fillmore of the United States of America, demanding the right to put up and trade at Japanese ports, be taken straight to the emperor, who, even if such a letter had ever reached him, would not have known what to do with it.

Communications with the Japanese were laborious, since the only European language known to their interpreters was Dutch. After Portuguese missionaries were banned from Japan in the seventeenth century, Dutch merchants, who were more interested in money than spreading the faith, were the only Europeans allowed to stay. The Japanese officials, though curious about American armaments and content to drink brandy and sugar on board Perry's flagship, were under instruction to tell the "flowery-flagged devils" to go away. They insisted that the only place to conduct business with foreigners was Nagasaki. But Perry, confident in the power of his guns, refused to budge. The Reverend Samuel Wells Williams, the official American interpreter, whose grasp of Japanese was tenuous, wrote in his journal that "the universal Yankee nation" had come "to disturb [Japan's] apathy and long ignorance."

When, after long deliberations, during which the Japanese countered Perry's imperious behavior with polite vagueness and other stalling tactics, Perry was finally allowed to go ashore, the two sides set out to impress each other with as much pomp as they could muster. The commodore strode forth, flanked by his two tallest black bodyguards. The Japanese were dressed in their finest silks. Presents were exchanged: rich brocades, porcelain bowls, lacquer boxes, fans, and other finely worked treasures for the Americans; a telegraph and a miniature train for the Japanese. The Japanese brought on some sumo wrestlers, whose stomachs Perry was invited to punch. Many toasts were drunk, and one of the Japanese officials, after consuming large amounts of whiskey and champagne, threw his arms around the commodore and said, in the common fashion of Japanese men celebrating international friendship in a drunken state: "Nippon and America, all the same heart."

Williams, a cool man of the cloth, noted that it was indeed "a curious mélange" of East and West, "railroads and telegraph, boxers and educated athlete . . . shaven pates and nightgowns, soldiers with muskets and drilling in close array, soldiers with petticoats, sandals, two swords, and all in disorder, like a crowd—all these things and many other things, exhibiting the difference between our civilization and usages and those of this secluded, pagan people." The Japanese gifts were clearly those of a "partially enlightened people," while the American presents showed "the success of science and enterprise" of "a higher civilization."

Twenty years later, many Japanese would take the same view, as though the "universal" West had come to bring light to a nation sunk in medieval darkness.

Commodore Perry may indeed have been convinced that his was a mission of enlightenment of lesser breeds, but his more immediate concern, on this and on a second mission in 1854, was to further the interests of American trade. The sixty-one guns on the decks of his ships, and the woefully unprepared Japanese coastal defenses (most cannon were fake, and there was no Japanese navy), finally convinced the shogun's government in Edo that compromise was preferable to a suicidal war. Henceforth, American ships were permitted to enter two designated Japanese ports and load up on coal and other supplies, for which they would pay as a first step toward establishing trade relations.

All this was hugely gratifying from an American point of view, and Commodore Perry would be remembered in history as the man who "opened" Japan, a distinction that Perry himself was the first to claim and widely trumpet during his lifetime. It is true that Perry's black ships, as well as other Western vessels lurking in the neighborhood, provoked a political crisis in Japan that led to the end of self-imposed isolation. The vulnerability of the Edo *bakufu*, whose autocratic rule had lasted more than two centuries, was shown up by superior foreign force, rather in the way that Japanese armies exposed the fragility of European empires in World War II. The Japanese were deeply divided about the best way to respond. Some factions, in a minority, had argued for some time to let the foreigners in and open Japan to trade. Others were in favor of rejecting the barbarians at any cost. A growing number of disgruntled provincial samurai and intellectuals were plotting to bring down the discredited *bakufu* and place the emperor (and themselves) at the center of a more vigorous state. Militant hotheads on the other side sought to cut down any opposition to the shogun. Perry alone was not responsible for creating all this ferment, but his actions surely brought things to a head.

However, Perry's assumption of Japanese ignorance could not have been further from the truth. At the time of his arrival in Edo Bay, the Japanese elite knew more about America than Americans knew about Japan. Indeed, despite their relative isolation, the Japanese knew more about the West than most other Asians did, including the Chinese. The extent of their knowledge of American and British politics, of Western science, medicine, history, and geography, was truly remarkable. They had detailed maps of the United States. They knew about U.S. political institutions. Western science had been introduced in the seventeenth century. Studies had been made of the Russian military, the British economy, and much more besides. More important, however, in light of things to come, were the conclusions Japanese drew from their studies.

———

It is often assumed that Christianity never had a chance in Japan. In fact, sixteenth-century Spanish and Portuguese missionaries were so successful in converting Japanese, especially among the elite, that the shoguns and their house intellectuals developed a deep fear of the Western faith. Japanese converts were massacred in 1638, foreign missionaries expelled, and all foreign books assumed to contain a Christian message banned, including scientific books by Matteo Ricci and, more oddly, Euclid's *Elements* and Cicero's *On Friendship*. But this didn't bring Western learning to a halt. The banning of presumed Christian propaganda in the early seventeenth century, and the presence of the Dutch merchants in Nagasaki, led to the emergence of *Rangaku*, Dutch learning. The students of this new discipline were called *Rangakusha*, or Dutch scholars.

The popular image of the Dutch was that of exotic beasts, who lifted their legs, like dogs, when they relieved themselves. Their hair was red and their eyes a devilish blue. But the official translators in Nagasaki, who also acted as state security agents, rather like the official guides in communist countries a few centuries later, quickly noticed the effectiveness of Western medicine and by implication the inadequacies of Chinese methods. Without dictionaries or grammars, they learned to read Dutch, an extraordinary intellectual achievement, and a number of physicians in Nagasaki and Edo became diligent scholars of European medical science. There was some official interest in Dutch matters, too. Once a year Dutch merchants were summoned to Edo, where the shogun and his entourage would pump them with questions and, for their amusement, ask them to sing songs, dance, kiss one another, and generally perform like circus animals.

In 1720, the ban on Western books was relaxed by the shogun, Tokugawa Yoshimune, who took a more serious interest in European affairs. He had an unusually open mind, but he was also a traditional ruler who felt responsible, like Chinese emperors, for agricultural prosperity. It was a time of commercial growth in the cities and violent rural unrest. To prevent more peasant riots, Yoshimune sought to improve life on the land. Since time is an essential factor in agriculture, the shogun was concerned about the calendar. After being advised that Europeans had a more accurate way of measuring time than the Chinese, he decided to encourage Dutch learning. "People of the red-hair country," he said, "customarily do things by mental reckoning and by reason; they only use implements they can see; if a fact is not certain, they do not say so, and they do not make use of it. . . ."

Although Yoshimune's interest in Dutch learning was practical more than philosophical, his attitude was quite different from that of Chinese emperors, who conceived of their celestial empire as the center of the world. His successors were not always as curious and broad-minded, and Dutch learning remained a precarious business, especially in the early nineteenth century, when the government cracked down on heterodox teachings. No matter how patriotic and even conservative most Dutch scholars were, a faint suspicion of treachery hung over those who showed too keen an interest in foreign matters. The authorities—and most scholars, too—took the line that although Western science might be a useful tool to rule Japan more effectively, foreign thinking should be kept far from common minds, lest the people get "confused" and forget to obey their rulers.

The ideology of the Tokugawa *bakufu* was neo-Confucianism, a particularly conservative strand of Confucianism devised in the twelfth century by a Chinese philosopher named Chu Hsi, who stressed the importance of natural order and, in the Japanese interpretation, absolute obedience to authority. The role of official Confucian scholars was to define the dogma and make sure people adhered to it. They were like clerics, empowered to interpret the rules of heaven. The great liberal nineteenth-century educator Fukuzawa Yukichi described the limits of this tradition well: "In our country, learning has meant learning belonging to the world of the rulers; it has been no more than a branch of the government." Many of these Confucianists, or *jusha,* were teachers and doctors of Chinese medicine. Western learning, which contradicted some of their most cherished beliefs, was a direct threat to their status, so it was in their interest to see its promoters cut down to size.

Getting too close to foreign teachers could have tragic consequences. One of the most scholarly members of the Dutch trade mission in Nagasaki was a dour physician of German origin named Philipp Franz von Siebold. A voracious collector of things Japanese, von Siebold had many devoted Japanese disciples. On a trip to Edo in 1826, he exchanged gifts with Takahashi Kageyasu, the distinguished interpreter and student of astronomy known to the Dutch as Globius. Von Siebold received a map of Japan, and Globius was given a naval map of the world. As soon as news of this exchange leaked out, von Siebold was arrested for spying and later expelled, while Globius died in prison three years later, possibly by his own hand.

Another unfortunate scholar was a young man named Yoshida Shoin, who was so desperate to learn more about the Western world that he begged Commodore Perry to take him back to America on his ship. Perry refused. Yoshida was arrested for embarking on this adventure and locked up in a cage. His teacher, Sakuma Shozan, who had developed theories, based on his Western knowledge, on the best ways to defend Japan against foreign incursions, was imprisoned for encouraging his pupil to study overseas. He wrote a famous treatise, entitled *Reflection on My Errors*. After his release, he was murdered by anti-Western fanatics for riding his horse on a European-style saddle.

Foreign learning, then, could be dangerous. But most Dutch scholars, even those who advocated a compromise solution to the foreign crisis provoked by Perry's arrival, were hardly political rebels. Most were too careful, or too indifferent, to be involved in political affairs. Almost all were ardent patriots anyway, who believed in the neo-Confucian rules of obedience even as they criticized Sino-centric obscurantism. Globius, the same man who exchanged gifts with Philipp von Siebold and died as a suspected traitor, had advised his government in 1825 to drive away all foreign ships from the Japanese coast. It would be nice if one could divide Japanese thinkers of the eighteenth and nineteenth (or indeed twentieth) centuries into progressive, liberal, democratic Westernizers on the one side and reactionary, nativist authoritarians on the other. But that is not the way it was or is. The keenest promoters of trade and compromise—there were many Dutch scholars among them—still argued that one day, when Japan had learned enough from the barbarians to resist them, the country could safely be closed again.

—

Even if the students of Dutch science were not aware of it themselves, their knowledge helped to undermine the philosophical legitimacy of the Confucian state. The Japanese had borrowed a Chinese concept of statecraft based on cosmic principles: The natural order of human society followed the natural order of the cosmos, and a benevolent ruler had to make sure they remained in harmony. Confucian ethics were believed to be in line with the principles of nature. Dutch learning introduced an entirely different view of the world. If the principles of nature could be analyzed through reason, and the cosmology underpinning the Confucian state refuted by science, this would constitute a serious challenge to political legitimacy.

The impact of Western science in China was, if anything, more serious than in Japan, for it showed that China was not the center of the universe. The Chinese way to stave off the consequences of what might have been an ethical revolution was to separate Chinese ethics from Western science, as though European ideas had no ethical implications. A popular saying in the late nineteenth century was "Chinese learning for the essential principles, Western learning for the practical applications." In fact, it never really worked in China. Western learning couldn't be reduced to mere technology without gross distortion, and the old Sino-centric principles were hard to reconcile with scientific inquiry. This is why Chinese thinkers since the nineteenth century have tended to lurch from sullen conservatism to violent iconoclasm. Either the Chinese tradition, whatever it was supposed to be, had to be defended against the merest speck of foreign pollution or every vestige of it had to be smashed in the name of science. The history of communist China is an illustration of both.

The Japanese response to Western ideas was similar but less traumatic, or at least it was traumatic in a different way. Japanese intellectuals, too, used the face-saving formula "Western science, Japanese essence." It never quite worked in Japan, either, but Japan had the great advantage of being in the cultural borderlands. Japanese thinkers could shift fairly easily from seeing China as the center of wisdom to finding another center of orientation. The point was that few Japanese had illusions about the world revolving around Japan. They may have thought Japan was uniquely favored as a divinely blessed land, but it was one land competing with many others. They also knew that their political system, and the principles upon which it was based, had been imported from China, and there was nothing to stop them from borrowing from somewhere else when the old order was no longer working.

Another important difference with China was the separation of powers. In China, both secular and political power were concentrated in the imperial court. In Tokugawa Japan, the shogun ran the country like a military strongman, while the emperor was more like a pope, whose blessing was used to legitimate the secular rulers. This arrangement was somewhat complicated by the fact that the shoguns, who belonged to a dynasty as much as the emperors, began to acquire imperial trappings of their own. But the separation of powers had one great advantage. It was possible to rebel against the government, especially if it was done in the name of loyalty to the emperor, without seeming to be unpatriotic. The same was not so easy in China.

Western influence has often been a catalyst for radical change in Japan, but it was by no means the only reason the *bakufu* system began to look threadbare. Already in the seventeenth century an increasingly wealthy and sophisticated merchant class had developed in coastal cities, especially Osaka. They traded in commodities, entered into free contracts, and speculated on futures markets. As the merchants, who were officially classified as a lower caste than peasants and artisans, got richer, the samurai, nominally at the top of the caste system, often became useless and, in the eighteenth and nineteenth centuries, progressively poorer. What was a professional warrior to do in times of peace? There were far too many samurai to give them all government jobs, and to engage in business was beneath their dignity. The romantic tracts, which became so popular in the West three hundred years later, about warrior codes and samurai chivalry were really a sign of idleness. The caste system, aimed at keeping the samurai on top and the merchants in their place, was out of step with economic developments. And the policy of national isolation cut Japan off from technological progress.

News of the disastrous Opium Wars in the 1840s came as a shock, for it not only proved how backward China had become, it showed Japan's own vulnerability. In fact, however, many Japanese had suspected as much long before that. After barbarian Manchus had toppled the Ming dynasty in 1644, the Middle Kingdom began to lose much of its prestige. Around the time that the free-spirited shogun Tokugawa Yoshimune encouraged Dutch studies, there was a revival of interest in Japanese cultural traditions. Nativist scholars looked for (and found) proof of Japanese superiority in ancient Japanese poetry, Shinto animism, and emperor worship. Some even replaced China with Japan as the true Middle Kingdom—in their own minds, at least. Chinese dynastic politics, with its rebellions and upheavals, was contrasted unfavorably with the purity of the Japanese imperial line. Chinese learning was thought to be coldly rationalistic compared to the delicacy of Japanese literary expression. Even Japanese Sinophiles began to challenge the notion that neo-Confucianism reflected the natural order. And the introduction of geography, through Dutch learning, made it quite clear that China was not the center of the world.

—

Japanese nativists, to this day, have the irritating habit of studying foreign ideas to confirm the unique superiority of their own nation. Shinto revivalists seized upon Copernican astronomy as proof that the Japanese had been right all along. Of course the earth revolves around the sun. Was Amaterasu, the sun goddess, not the divine ancestor of the Japanese people? Had Japan not been heliocentric from the very beginning? This was anathema to Buddhists and Sino-centric conservatives, of course, and precisely why Western ideas excited Japanese nativists: They helped to emancipate Japan from the Chinese cultural orbit.

Even more interesting was the use some nativists made of Christianity. The center of nativist scholarship in the late eighteenth and early nineteenth centuries was an academy set in a handsome compound (still there today) in Mito, a town to the northeast of Edo. Mito had long been a center of learning. The lord of the domain at the time of Commodore Perry's arrival was a hawkish figure who resisted any compromise with foreigners. He promoted the slogan "Respect the emperor, expel the barbarians." Under his auspices the so-called Mito School specialized in theories of Japanese uniqueness. One of its leading lights was Aizawa Seishisai, who wrote a famous tract in 1825 entitled *New Theses*. Aizawa argued that Christianity was evil and Western barbarians were "wild boars and wolves" who should be exterminated as soon as they hit Japanese shores.

Yet Aizawa and his Mito colleagues were diligent students of Dutch learning. Aizawa concluded that the superior strength of European nations, which he was swift to recognize, was due to the Western faith. Christianity, as a state religion, he thought, made European subjects naturally obedient to their rulers. Belief in one God, he said, created national unity. State and church should go together. What Japan needed, then, was its own state religion, with the emperor as its highest priest. To this end, Shinto, as the most ancient Japanese creed, would be transformed from a nature cult with many gods to a national faith that welded all Japanese together under one imperial roof. The sun goddess, as the sacred ancestor, would be worshiped as though she were an equivalent of the Christian God. Regrettably, the merging of church and state was to be one of the foundations of modern Japanese nationalism. The appeal was to ancient tradition, but the model was European.

In their implicit or explicit challenges to the old Sino-centric order, the students of Western learning and the Mito nativists were really on the same side. Neither the *Rangakusha* nor the nativists welcomed the arrival of Perry's ships. Many were out-and-out xenophobes. But they recognized the power of Western ideas and wished to learn more, so Japan could one day compete with the best of them. In many ways, the nativists, despite all their mumbo jumbo about ancient texts, purity of imperial bloodlines, and ancestral gods, were as modern as the Westernizers, even though the West often came to them in a highly distorted fashion. And they managed to pick some of the worst, most bellicose aspects of the Western world for emulation in Japan.

One of them was colonialism. A remarkable student of Dutch learning in the late eighteenth century was the son of an impoverished samurai named Honda Toshiaki, also known to his admirers as "the Japanese Benjamin Franklin." The Japanese Benjamin Franklin actually enjoyed close relations with the Mito School. He had, it is true, some very progressive ideas for his time. Government should be based on popular consent, he said, for "when the country is ruled by force against the will of the people, many in their hearts oppose this compulsion and become criminals." He was also in favor of foreign travel to broaden Japanese knowledge, and he blamed most of his country's problems on scientific ignorance and slavish copying of discredited Chinese ways. He even proposed abolishing the Chinese writing system. His study of Britain led him to conclude that a small maritime nation needed to trade with foreigners. He believed that Japan urgently needed four things: gunpowder, metals, shipping, and colonization.

Without a colonial empire, Honda argued, a nation could not achieve greatness. His visions of Japan's colonial enterprise were, like his politics, both progressive and ruthless, rather like those of his favorite model, Britain. The natives in colonized lands could be exploited for labor and natural resources used to enrich Japan. Wooded lands could be stripped of lumber, a remarkably prescient description of Japanese activities in Southeast Asia today. His view of good colonial rule was equally ahead of its time: "It

is the task of the ruler-father to direct and educate the natives in such a manner that there will not be a single one of
them who spends even one unproductive day."

Commodore Perry's interpreter, the good Reverend Williams, then, had rather missed the point about the Japanese
"natives." They were far from being apathetic or ignorant,
as he thought. Japanese had plenty of ideas, many of them
arriving from the West long before Williams. The question was which ideas would stick, as the old order tottered
and a new, modern state began to take shape. History was
not made by scholars, even though their ideas had consequences. Honda's ideas were fully appreciated only in the
1920s, when his reputation was higher than it had been in
his own lifetime. But the men who helped to bring down
the *bakufu* were inspired by ideas as well as self-interest.
Some were xenophobes, some protoliberals, and some a bit
of both.

If xenophobia, authoritarianism, and war marked much
of the coming century, the road to more open, democratic
arrangements was not completely blocked. One of the foreign words to have crept into the Japanese vocabulary
around 1837 (through a Dutch biography of Napoleon)
was *vrijheit,* "liberty," which at least one Japanese translator
would never forget. He knew it was dangerous to say it out
loud. This depressed him, so according to a contemporary
witness, he would drink to lift his spirits. But "when he was
drunk he could not keep from shouting *'Vrijheit!'* "

Perhaps Williams's view of the Japanese as "partially
enlightened" was not so wrong after all. The same applies
to all people in the world. The enlightened side has to
struggle everywhere, at all times. In Japan, alas, the battle
was too often lost.

—

The period from 1853 to 1868, from Perry's arrival to the overthrow of the shogunate, is known in Japanese as *bakumatsu*, or "end of *bakufu*." *Bakumatsu* shares the giddy, somewhat salacious connotations of "fin de siècle," but it also has a darker, more violent image, expressed in brilliantly sinister Kabuki plays and, much later, in countless swordfight movies. The end of *bakufu* was a time of violent intrigues and murderous plots, of rebellions and countercoups, of feudal lords from the southwest maneuvering against the Tokugawa loyalists, ending in civil war. It was a time of popular hysteria and millenarian cults. Mobs gathered in the big cities, including Edo itself, carrying Shinto images, visiting shrines, dancing half-naked in the streets, having sex in public, and raiding wealthy houses, while shouting in a state of quasi-religious ecstasy: "It's okay, it's okay, anything we do is okay!" The 1860s, like the 1930s and the early 1970s, produced many young extremists, who saw ultraviolence as the way to national salvation, the result, perhaps, of a society that in more stable times tends to be too tightly controlled.

Commodore Perry's arrival turned the slogan "Respect the emperor, expel the barbarians" into an anti-*bakufu* war cry. The increasingly helpless government in Edo was blamed for the foreign intrusions on Japanese soil. People feared change but rebelled against tradition. Revolutionaries were at once iconoclastic and reactionary. Young extremists, often of lower samurai stock, who had lost their moorings in the old society, expressed their xenophobic, emperor-worshiping, nation-saving idealism in a spate of assassinations, which set the pattern for the next century. In 1858, a senior *bakufu* official signed a treaty giving the United States trading and residency rights. He knew he had no choice. Two years later, he was ambushed outside the shogun's castle in Edo by a group of samurai from Mito who pulled him from his palanquin and slashed off his head. To make up for this necessary act of insubordination, the assassin later disemboweled himself in the ritual manner of his warrior caste.

Another would-be assassin was a young man from the Tosa region (in the southwestern island of Shikoku) named Sakamoto Ryoma. The hero of many novels, plays, television dramas, and films, he is usually depicted as a Japanese Garibaldi who began as a wild-haired protohippie with a sword. This kind of thing has been more widely admired since World War II than in less liberal periods. But Sakamoto's political journey from murderous fanaticism to political enlightenment contains all the dark glamour, radical intelligence, and openness to different political possibilities of his age.

Bored with the prospect of a constrained provincial samurai life, Sakamoto dropped out of school, left his family and his lord, and joined a fencing academy. With a head full of Mito School propaganda about national purity and the barbarian peril, Sakamoto then set off to assassinate traitors. He thought he had found the perfect target in Katsu Rintaro, the *bakufu*'s naval specialist and a renowned Dutch scholar. Katsu had spent time in Nagasaki with Dutch naval experts and seen American strength with his own eyes as a member of the first Japanese mission to the United States in 1859. He concluded that Japan's only chance to survive as an independent nation was to open its borders. To a crazed young warrior like Sakamoto, this smacked of cowardice and treachery.

The story goes that Katsu, confronted by his young assassin, kept his cool and said: "Did you come to kill me? If you did, you ought to wait until we've had a chance to talk." What followed was one of those extraordinary volte-faces that sometimes mark the overheated behavior of Japanese heroes. Katsu explained that he was a patriot like Sakamoto, and his only goal was to strengthen Japan. The best way to fight the barbarians, he said, was to learn all their tricks first. Hence his advocacy of openness and ini-tial compromise. According to legend, Sakamoto dropped his sword, fell on his knees, apologized for his "narrow-minded bigotry," and begged Katsu to take him as his disci-ple. Perhaps something like that actually occurred.

Sakamoto served Katsu for several years and went on to play a diplomatic role in forging links between Choshu, Satsuma, and Tosa, the main southwestern fiefdoms in op-position to the *bakufu*. Satsuma was in the south of Kyushu, and Choshu was at the western tip of Honshu. Being on the losing side in the civil wars around the turn of the seven-teenth century, the lords of these domains had never been in the inner circles of Tokugawa power. The leaders of Satsuma and Choshu were ready to go to war with the Edo government, but Sakamoto advocated a more peaceful so-lution and urged his allies to persuade the shogun to resign as the ruler. Sakamoto proposed that Japan should be gov-erned by a council of feudal lords, in which the Tokugawa shogun could still play a role, but not as the supreme leader. In 1867, the last shogun agreed to this proposition. But the warriors of Satsuma and Choshu were impatient. Nothing less than the fall of the Tokugawa house would satisfy them.

Sakamoto's new base of operations was Nagasaki, where he studied Western political systems. He was particularly interested in European constitutions. Though poorly edu-cated, Sakamoto must have had a brilliant mind, for in

1867 he came up with a highly sophisticated blueprint for the post-*bakufu* state. Political power should be returned to the imperial court. But all government measures would be decided "on the basis of general opinion" in two legislative bodies, an upper and lower house. A constitution would be drawn up, and high office would be reserved for "men of ability" and no longer based on caste or rank. (One should remember that even lowly samurai like Sakamoto were required to grovel to their superiors, in their own as well as other fiefs.) Later, in another document, Sakamoto elaborated how such worthies would be chosen through election committees. Foreign affairs "should be carried on according to appropriate regulations worked out on the basis of general opinion."

Given Sakamoto's own background and the fact that politics of this kind had never existed in Japan before, this was a remarkable document. Much of its language was adopted a year later in the Charter Oath of the Meiji Restoration, which brought *bakufu* rule to an end. Meiji, literally "Enlightened Rule," was the name of the new imperial reign. It would soon become synonymous with an astonishing race for modernity, watched with awe by Asians who were still living under Western colonial rule.

An inspiring story, then, of a society transformed by progressive ideas from feudalism and military autocracy to liberty and enlightenment. Alas, it was not quite so simple. The seeds of political liberalism had been sown, to be sure, but their growth was hampered from the beginning by other measures, moving Japan in the opposite direction. Once the emperor and his courtiers were harnessed directly to a political cause, as they were by the anti-*bakufu* rebels, mostly from Satsuma and Choshu, a particularly modern kind of authoritarianism emerged.

—

For many centuries, the emperors in Kyoto had played a symbolic role as guardians of Japanese culture and ethics. Their political blessing was taken for granted by the shoguns, who rarely even bothered to visit them, let alone consult them on matters of state. This changed drastically in the late 1850s, when Emperor Komei was urged by anti-*bakufu* hard-liners to oppose a treaty with the United States. This was not the kind of thing emperors were supposed to express opinions about. Even if the anti-*bakufu* rebels did not actually wish to see the emperor take direct political power, they had begun to politicize the imperial institution.

The consequences of this ultimately disastrous course could already be seen in early drafts of the new constitution, drawn up by Sakamoto Ryoma, among others. After a meeting between Satsuma and Tosa representatives in Kyoto in 1867, a document was drafted with the following sentence: "There cannot be two rulers in a land, or two heads in a house, and it is most reasonable to return administration and justice to one ruler." The wording is still sufficiently vague to leave some room for secular government. The emperor could still be a ruler in name, while a civilian government actually governed. But it began to look as though the Shinto revivalist motto *saisei ichi*, the unity of government and religious rites, would be turned into a political reality.

The end of *bakufu* government did not come as peacefully as Sakamoto had envisaged. Civil war raged in 1868–1869 between *bakufu* loyalists and imperial armies. The former came from the northeastern domains and the latter from the southwest. The fighting was brutal, and civilians unlucky enough to be caught in between were treated with typical samurai contempt. The *bakufu*'s last stand was in Aizu, a castle town to the northeast of Mito. For more than two weeks, the lord of Aizu stood his ground against thirty thousand imperial troops, who blasted his castle with the latest Western guns. The town was burned to the ground. Dozens of loyalist young samurai slit their stomachs in despair. The castle fell. The Aizu lord lost three thousand men. And the rest of his twenty thousand–odd men were chased into the barren north, where many died of starvation.

The emperor was moved to Edo, now renamed Tokyo, and for the first time in almost a thousand years, the emperor and the government shared the same capital. A shrine, named Yasukuni, was built in the center of Tokyo to commemorate the men who had died for the imperial cause. Their enshrined souls, like those of millions who died in a succession of later wars, were worshiped there, unlike the poor souls of men who had remained loyal to the *bakufu*, for whom there was no sacred site. Yasukuni shrine still manages to stir up deep antipathy, not only among Japan's former enemies in Asia, but among Christians and liberals in Japan itself.

Sakamoto, sad to say, did not live to see the final demise of Tokugawa rule and the Meiji Restoration he had done so much to prepare. In the last years of the *bakufu*, Kyoto had become a wild place filled with plotters, assassins, and roaming swordsmen, all looking for trouble. In the winter of 1867, Sakamoto was hiding out in the house of a friendly soy sauce merchant. He knew that *bakufu* gangs were out to get him but thought he was safe enough to send his bodyguards out for some food. A stranger knocked on the merchant's door and said he was looking for Sakamoto Ryoma. Sakamoto's servant turned to inform his master upstairs. But before he could do so, the visitor rushed in with two other swordsmen, and slashed Sakamoto's head, body, and limbs. The assassins were members of the Shinsengumi, the armed militia formed to kill all enemies of the shogun. After they had gone, the man who wrote the first draft of the Japanese constitution lay dead in a pool of blood.

2

CIVILIZATION AND
ENLIGHTENMENT

February 11, 1889, the anniversary of the date on which Japan's mythical first emperor is alleged to have founded the imperial line, was the chosen date for Japan to take its rightful place among the world's great nations. New, resolutely postfeudal Japan was to have its first constitution as a badge of "Civilization and Enlightenment," or *Bunmei Kaika,* that great slogan of the Meiji era. There was another slogan, too, which came into fashion a bit later: *Fukoku Kyohei,* meaning "Rich Country, Strong Army." But this is getting ahead of the story. The constitution would be handed down by the emperor to his subjects, as though it were a gift from the gods. The ceremonies surrounding this illustrious event were splendid and typical of Meiji Japan's peculiar cultural schizophrenia.

In the early morning, the Meiji emperor, known outside Japan as Emperor Mutsuhito, dressed up in ancient court dress and withdrew into the inner sanctum of the Shinto shrine at his Tokyo palace to inform his imperial ancestors of the new constitution. He explained that this document was in line with the "advance of civilization," then hastened to reassure his divine forebears that it would naturally preserve the imperial sovereignty they had bequeathed to him. More than preserve: The point of the Meiji Restoration—or of Meiji Restoration propaganda—was that it "restored" the ancient form of Japanese imperial rule.

The Meiji emperor's subjects were still ignorant of the contents of the constitution their emperor had so graciously bestowed. They would have remained in the dark even if they had attended the next ceremony, conducted later in the day, in the European style devised by the emperor's German adviser on enlightened court etiquette.

The emperor's Western-style throne room, as shown in a contemporary woodblock print, is a Victorian mishmash of lush European and Japanese motifs, with a preponderance of gold tassels, red plush, and ornate gilt candelabras. The emperor, who had changed into the uniform of a European field marshal, sits on a gilded Prussian armchair, with the imperial crest behind him and a red carpet stretching beneath him. The empress, whose presence on such a public occasion was another sign of Japan's new enlightened and civilized style, sits at his feet, wearing a rather unbecoming pink evening gown. The emperor's ministers and other bearded and bewhiskered dignitaries, in frock coats and military uniforms, stand unnaturally tall and are blessed by the print artist with slightly longer legs than reality might have warranted. On one side of the emperor is the diplomatic corps, looking on with obvious approval, like parents at a school play. In attendance, too, is Ito Hirobumi, president of the Privy Council and the main author of the constitution. Ito was an admirer of Bismarck and affected some of the Iron Chancellor's mannerisms, including the way he held his cigar. (Yoshida Shigeru, the post–World War II prime minister, would one day pay the same compliment to Winston Churchill.)

One blot on this joyous occasion was the assassination of Mori Arinori, the reforming education minister, who was so convinced of the superiority of Western civilization that he proposed mixed marriages with people of European stock as the best way forward for Japan. Xenophobes had long hated his Westernizing ways. He was murdered on Constitution Day by an ex-samurai from Choshu for not paying sufficient respect to the holiest imperial Shinto shrine at Ise. While Mori would go down in history as a

rather earnest pedagogue, his young killer became a popular figure because of the "sincerity" of his patriotic spirit.

So now they had it, a real constitution, after having been
promised one in 1868. For a decade, people all over Japan
had discussed the nature and possible contents of a constitution. Advocates for civil liberties and natural rights had
made proposals and written drafts. Ueki Emori, a former
samurai from Tosa, like Sakamoto Ryoma, had composed a
song to promote popular sovereignty, containing such stirring lines as these:

> Let's resolve for constitutional laws
> And for the early popular election of an assembly.
> Onward! Onward! People of our country.
> Let's push for liberty and people's rights.

What they had got, however, was a vaguely worded document that put sovereignty entirely into imperial hands. Like
the uniforms and top hats worn by Japanese worthies, and
like some of the modern redbrick buildings erected in the
center of Tokyo, the constitution had a respectable Western-
style veneer. Based on the Prussian constitution, it was meant
to impress the Western world that Japan was now a modern
nation-state, which should be free at last of the unequal
treaties that still afforded Americans and Europeans special
privileges on Japanese soil, such as their own law courts. The
old game of catch-up with an outside metropole was being
replayed as it had been for centuries, with one difference:
Paris, London, Berlin, and Washington had replaced the old
capitals of China.

The Meiji constitution did allow for parliamentary,
or Diet, elections, the first of which were to take place the

following year, but political parties would have no say in the selection of government ministers. Only a small percentage of the population—for the most part wealthy landowners—would have the right to vote. Ito Hirobumi, a relatively free-spirited figure among his peers, agreed entirely with his role model, Otto von Bismarck, that popular sovereignty would be a very dangerous thing. "Because imperial sovereignty is the cornerstone of our constitution," he said, "our system is not based on the European ideas in force in some European countries of joint rule of the king and the people."

Ito and his fellow oligarchs, mostly from Satsuma and Choshu, had spent much time after the 1868 restoration shopping around for good political ideas. They went on missions to Europe and the United States. They studied British and American models and made sentimental visits to Holland, as Japan's "oldest friend." Although they admired American strength and appreciated the friendliness of their reception in that country, American democracy worried them. It smacked of disorder. So they were relieved to hear from the Japanese resident in Germany that there were other alternatives, more suitable to Japan. Germanophilia was not universal. One famous Meiji leader, Okuma Shigenobu, was an advocate of British constitutional thought. But this avenue was swiftly blocked by his colleagues, and Okuma almost lost his life in an assassination attempt by the same kind of sincere zealot who brought down Mori Arinori.

Japanese democracy, then, as defined in the Meiji constitution, was a sickly child from the beginning. The spirit of the constitution was a mixture of German and traditional Japanese authoritarianism. But the greatest danger, in the long run, lay in its vagueness. For the emperor, though empowered with absolute sovereignty, was not really a royal generalissimo. He was never a dictator in the European sense. The emperor was not supposed to be directly involved in politics; he was expected to stand above worldly affairs, while a bureaucratic elite made political decisions in his name. At the same time, Japan's armed services owed their loyalty only to the monarch and not to the civilian government. This made for a politics of veils and smoke screens, behind which power could be exercised more or less unchecked, without any individual having to take final responsibility for his actions.

Could it have been otherwise? Did the Japanese have to pick a quasi-Teutonic, pseudoancient Japanese authoritarian system? Was there even a chance of establishing a more democratic system? A chance, yes. But given the men who forced the Tokugawa *bakufu* out of power, it was never likely.

The heroes of the Meiji Restoration, notably Ito Hirobumi, Saigo Takamori, Yamagata Aritomo, Okubo Toshimichi, and Kido Takayoshi, all from Choshu or Satsuma, were steeped in the samurai ethos of loyalty, obedience, and military discipline. Saigo Takamori, one of the most romantic figures of the restoration, a large fighting man celebrated for the impressive size of his testicles, wanted to establish a warrior state in Satsuma. He became a hero to disaffected samurai, who felt left behind by modern reforms, most significantly the abolition of the samurai's status as a hereditary caste, and in 1877 he led a bloody rebellion against the central government. The ostensible cause of the Satsuma rebellion was Japanese policy toward Korea, which Saigo deemed too soft. But the real point was that even reforms that were still far from democratic went too far for many thousands of men, who were used to more feudal ways. It is a clear sign of the traditional Japanese fondness for reactionary rebels that Saigo, whose sincerity was never in doubt, is still seen as a greater hero than some of his more liberal-minded colleagues.

What is surprising about early Meiji history is not that Satsuma and Choshu autocrats found popular sovereignty uncongenial, but that so many Japanese took the opposite view. The Charter Oath, issued by the emperor in 1868, promised that "deliberative councils" would be established and "all matters decided by public discussions." Prominent figures from the old Tosa domain, following the lead of Sakamoto Ryoma and spurred on by such inspirational literature as Samuel Smiles's *Self-Help*, formed societies to promote representative politics. Since these Tosa men were excluded from the central government dominated by leaders from Satsuma and Choshu, it was in their interest to do so. They wanted to represent themselves.

In some ways, early Meiji Japan was like China in the 1980s and 1990s: Economic reforms were not matched by political ones. More than that, Ito Hirobumi, among others, was convinced that too many political reforms would derail the progressive economic policies. Japan in the 1870s had the beginnings of a modern market economy. Caste differences were legally abolished; farmers could own their own land; people were free to buy property; and some monopolies were abolished in favor of free enterprise. But free enterprise was never free from state interference. As the Meiji slogan said, the point was to build up not just a rich country, but a powerful one, which meant government support for strategic industries needed by a strong army. Already in the last years of the Tokugawa shogunate, Japanese, helped by European experts, had started to build steamships and cannon. The first iron foundry was constructed in 1857. But it was in the 1880s, when the cash-strapped government sold off textile factories, railroads, cement plants, and other industries to private entrepreneurs, that Japan had its first real industrial boom. This means that Japan's industrial revolution came later than Britain's, but only a few years after that of Germany. Since only a few were brave enough in the beginning to risk taking on modern enterprises, much of Japan's industrial wealth was concentrated in a few companies that soon grew into the huge industrial combines known as *zaibatsu*. Mitsui, for example, grew from an Edo textile store to a massive concern of banks, trading companies, collieries, chemical plants, and much else besides. Another famous combine, Mitsubishi, began as a small shipping firm and by the 1930s was one of the biggest concerns in the world. Their growth followed a now familiar pattern in Japan. Instead of encouraging competition among big businesses in an unfettered marketplace, an intricate network of bureaucrats, politicians, and business leaders promoted industrial growth through strategic policies, government subsidies, and mutually beneficial backroom deals. Meiji Japan had its share of Horatio Algers. The alienation from their village roots of country boys who made it in the big city was a favorite theme of Meiji novelists. But, unlike in America, individual fortunes were subordinate to the demands of the state. As in Bismarck's Germany, the economy was as much part of the nationalist endeavor in Japan as the politics.

Economically, then, Meiji Japan was becoming a modern nation. But government was still the preserve of a few ex-samurai from the southwest. They—Okubo, Yamagata, Ito, and the others—became known as the oligarchs. These were able, energetic, and in some cases brilliant men, but their jealous guardianship of power made sure that democracy was hampered at birth.

The oligarchy, however, did not go unchallenged. One of the first men who wished to translate economic into political liberties was a Tosa intellectual named Itagaki Daisuke. Like Okuma, the relatively liberal Meiji leader, he was the target of a failed assassination. As he crumpled to the ground at a public meeting in 1882 after being struck down by a fanatical police officer, he is said to have shouted the famous line "Even if Itagaki perishes, liberty will never die!" In fact, Itagaki survived in rather better shape than the liberties he promoted.

Itagaki and other leaders of the so-called People's Rights Movement argued that sovereignty should not be based on divine right—a direct attack on imperial rule. The idea of natural law was often invoked. Rousseau was much read by these early advocates of people's rights, along with Mill, Spencer, Bentham, and Tocqueville. The society of like-minded activists turned into a political party, the Jiyuto, or Freedom Party. Okuma and his fellow Anglophiles set up a rival party called the Kaishinto, the Constitutional Progressive Party. But their interest in European theory notwithstanding, Itagaki and his fellow activists were still samurai at heart, who never thought that the common people should participate directly in politics. There were always enough Westerners at hand to firm up such views. Ulysses S. Grant, on a much heralded visit to Tokyo, advised the Japanese government that the Japanese people could not handle too much freedom. And one of the heroes of people's rights activists, the English philosopher Herbert Spencer, the man who in earlier years advocated the right to rebel against oppressive government, was of the opinion that only absolute imperial rule suited the Japanese.

In fact, however, many people did try to participate in politics. The enthusiasm with which politics was discussed in villages and towns by people of all classes is particularly interesting, given the common belief, held in Japan as well as abroad, that the "conformist," "consensus-minded," "obedient" Japanese don't take to politics. Not only did rural people form their own political parties, but Meiji Japan was marked by a huge number of rebellions, directed less at the central government than against local bosses and landlords. The problem was arbitrary rule. You didn't need to have read John Stuart Mill or Adam Smith to resent it. In at least one instance, farmers were up against the imperial institution itself. Although the right to private property was one of the key tenets of the Meiji reforms, the government had decided to confiscate land from farmers in Nagano prefecture for conversion to imperial forestland. The farmers resisted for twenty-five years, arguing their case on legal grounds. In 1905, they were paid some money in compensation. They were lucky not to be locked up for sedition.

One of the most famous uprisings took place in the mountains around Chichibu, northeast of Tokyo, in 1884. Like most rebellions, it was rooted in the farmers' crippling debts—brought on, at least partly, by misguided government policies. Represented by amateur lawyers, some Freedom Party figures, angry schoolteachers, and the odd rabble-rousing rogue, they formed the Poor People's Party. When petitions to the authorities, village meetings, and negotiations with creditors met time and again with violent police repression, the farmers decided they wouldn't take it anymore. Armed with swords, hunting rifles, and bamboo spears, the farmers battled with government troops for ten days. They lost, of course. Three hundred were jailed, seven executed.

Horrified by these rebellions, the leaders of the two "liberal" parties quickly dissociated themselves from what they regarded as unruly mobs. This was a characteristic but futile move. Weakened and demoralized by constant government harassment, the parties themselves were dissolved in 1884, only to revive later in a rather emasculated form as promoters of corporate interests: the Freedom Party for the Mitsui combine, the Constitutional Progressive Party for Mitsubishi.

———

"Civilization and Enlightenment" always was more a cultural than a political slogan, a matter of style and appearances. But appearances count for a lot in Japan. There was a satirical Meiji saying that went: "Knock a head without a top-knot, and you hear the sound of *Bunmei Kaika*." As if wearing one's hair in the European style were a sign of superior breeding. Some Meiji leaders seriously believed that a display of European manners would persuade Western powers to give up the unequal treaties.

There was something priggish, as well as noble and absurd, about Meiji enlightenment. Even as some ancient and quasi-ancient customs were invented or revived to dress up modernization in nativist garb, there was a conscious effort to reject or clean up the recent past, especially if it might seem frivolous or plebeian in Western eyes. The Kabuki theater, for example, once a lively feature of the raffish pleasure quarters, was made respectable and turned into an increasingly stagnant classical tradition. The great Kabuki actor Ichikawa Danjuro IX opened a new theater in

Tokyo in 1872, dressed not, as he would have before, in a dashing kimono, but in white tie and tails. "The theater of recent years," he said in his speech, "has drunk up filth and smelled of the coarse and the mean. . . . I am deeply grieved by this fact, and in consultation with my colleagues I have resolved to clean away the decay."

While the stench of late Edo brothel districts was removed from the Kabuki, Western theater was introduced to civilize the urban elite. One of the pioneers in this genre was an ex-policeman and radical activist named Kawakami Otojiro. In 1901, he went on an extended tour of Europe and the United States with his wife, Sadako, a former geisha alleged to have been Ito Hirobumi's mistress. They presented to fascinated Europeans a rather phony version of Kabuki, and to fascinated audiences in Japan an equally phony version of Western theater. On one memorable occasion, Kawakami, playing Hamlet in Tokyo, entered the stage on a bicycle. To the audience, for whom Hamlet was as exotic, and modern, as the bicycle, this did not seem incongruous at all.

Another Meiji peculiarity was the fashion for eating large quantities of meat, which was a radical break with Buddhist taboos. But then Buddhism went through hard times. In the first years after the restoration, Shinto fanatics went about smashing Buddhist temples in an effort to purge Japan of its Chinese cultural traditions. The fashion for meat began when Fukuzawa Yukichi, one of the greatest Meiji intellectuals, suggested that eating meat would improve Japanese physiques. Soon meat eating was promoted as a way to achieve enlightenment.

Writing almost a century later, the novelist Mishima Yukio could still work himself into a rage about the superficial primness of the Meiji years. Prohibitions on public nudity, mixed bathing, and other embarrassing signs of "the coarse and the mean" stemmed less from native prudery than from fear of foreign disapproval. Mishima likened Meiji Japan to "an anxious housewife preparing to receive guests, hiding away in closets common articles of daily use and laying aside comfortable everyday clothes, hoping to impress the guests with the immaculate, idealized life of her household, without so much as a speck of dust in view."

This is a slight exaggeration. Most Japanese did not act like stage Europeans, and even members of the upper classes did so only in public. But when they did, they did it with gusto. The high tide of ostentatious Europeanized posturing, the icing on the cake of "Civilization and Enlightenment," as it were, was the great ball at the Deer Cry Pavilion, or Rokumeikan, hosted by the foreign minister, Inoue Kaoru, in honor of the emperor's birthday in 1885. Pierre Loti, the French author of *Madame Chrysanthemum,* was there. His observations were supercilious and probably quite accurate. The exterior of the pavilion, designed by a British architect in a mixture of high Victorian, French Empire, and Italian Renaissance styles, was likened by Loti to a provincial French spa. He thought the Japanese gentlemen, dressed up in suits of tails, looked like performing monkeys, and the ladies, lining the walls like tapestries in their hoops and flounces and satin trains, were, well, "remarkable." Doing their best to strike the proper European attitudes, gentlemen puffed Havana cigars and played whist, while others picked at the truffles and pâté and ice-cream sorbets laid out on the buffet tables. A French orchestra struck up operetta tunes, while a German band played polkas, mazurkas, and waltzes. Loti: "They danced quite properly, my Japanese in Parisian gowns. But one senses that it is something *drilled into* them that they perform like automatons, without any personal initiative. If by chance they lose the beat, they have to be stopped and started all over again."

It is easy to laugh at all this with Pierre Loti. But the intention behind the entertainment was serious. Inoue Kaoru was foreign minister in his friend Ito Hirobumi's cabinet. They hoped that rapid Westernization would make foreign powers treat Japan as an equal and thus agree to relinquish their privileges under the unequal treaties. The best way to acquire modern—that is, Western—forms was to be exposed as much as possible to the real thing; hence the creation of the Deer Cry Pavilion. It was to be the place where East and West could mingle at the highest level, over whist and the mazurka. To critics of this kind of thing, Ito's government became known as "the dancing cabinet."

When it became clear that Western diplomats and writers were quite willing to dance, but not to revise the treaties as a result of Inoue's hospitality, the foreign minister's star began to fade. His policy was discredited, and in 1889 the Deer Cry Pavilion was sold to a private club. A backlash against all the Westernizing had already begun by then. The building, alas, is no more.

———

Westernization was not all glitter and political calculation. Some Meiji intellectuals had managed to absorb European ideas in a way that could have turned Japan in a more liberal direction than it actually did. The life of Fukuzawa Yukichi represents much of what was best about Meiji culture, even though he, too, was not entirely free of the priggish tendency. Fukuzawa's role was, in his own words, to "become the sole functioning agent for the introduction of Western learning." He founded an academy in Tokyo to this purpose, which later became Keio University. His book introducing customs and mores of the Western world was such a best-seller that other publications in this vein became known as "Fukuzawa books." And in the true manner of a Confucian sage, he tried to set a moral example in his life as well as his works. Unlike most Confucian scholars, however, he sought to give the example of an individualist, a critical thinker, independent of power. Fukuzawa was one of the first—and still uncommon—examples of an independent Japanese intellectual. His skeptical views, unheard of in the neo-Confucian tradition, were staunchly antiauthoritarian. He knew that assassination was always "an unpleasant possibility" and was lucky to escape from the murderous intentions of his second cousin, an excitable, though no doubt sincere, product of the Mito School.

Born in 1835 as the son of a low-ranking samurai, Fukuzawa was introduced to Western learning through Dutch studies. He was shocked to discover, however, that the foreigners who began to arrive in Japan in the 1860s didn't understand a word of Dutch. So he learned English as well, joined missions to the United States and Europe, and set out "to open this 'closed' country of ours." He was often disappointed by his fellow countrymen, especially by their habit, as he saw it, of bending with every wind, like "rubber dolls," always anxious to appease authority. But he never stopped arguing for intellectual freedom. In 1874, together with Mori Arinori and other enlightenment intellectuals, Fukuzawa started a society called Meirokusha, to encourage free and open debate. Their views were published in a journal by the same name. These men were not antigovernment activists. On the contrary, most held positions in the government. But this early experiment in open political discussion did not last long. An antilibel and press

law, promulgated in 1875, was so restrictive of free speech
that the members decided to close the magazine. Another
law, four years later, making it illegal for public servants,
teachers, soldiers, farmers, and students to attend any political meetings, made the Meirokusha impossible, too. And
so began the long retreat of Japanese intellectuals from
public affairs. Like so many of their counterparts in Germany, the intelligentsia withdrew to tend their academic
or aesthetic gardens.

Fukuzawa watched the end of promised freedoms with
dismay, but he decided against an open protest. He took
"full account of the conditions," he wrote in his autobiography, but "kept it among my private papers." When a
friend urged him to speak out, Fukuzawa said: "I am now
over forty years old, and so are you. Let us remember this
and beware of hurting other men." It was an attitude repeated by future generations of Japanese intellectuals.
Something died in the 1870s, and with some notable exceptions, it never fully revived until 1945.

———

One of the strangest and most emotional passages in
Fukuzawa's life story is his joy about the 1895 war with
China. The Sino-Japanese conflict was over the domination
of Korea. The Koreans, though traditionally subservient to
the Chinese court, were divided between pro-Chinese and
pro-Japanese factions, and the assassination in Shanghai of
the leader of the pro-Japanese faction was what triggered
the war. It was not just a geopolitical battle, however, but
also a test of the two nations' modernity in military affairs.
The one with the most advanced weapons, the most efficient army, and the most up-to-date tactics would win, and
that nation, despite being outnumbered in warships and
troops, was Japan. Fukuzawa was so happy about Japan's

victory that he "could hardly refrain from rising up in delight." In fact, this was not all that strange. One aspect of "Civilization and Enlightenment" was a contempt for the backwardness of other Asians. Fukuzawa saw Chinese learning as a kind of cancer in Japanese society. Joining the West, in his view, would have to mean a rejection of Asia. If Japan had been part of the Chinese cultural world before, it should now become part of the enlightened West. Japan's victory in the Sino-Japanese War showed how far the nation had "progressed." It was indeed a sign of a higher civilization. The popular woodblock prints of the war invariably show the Japanese soldiers as tall, pale-skinned, heroic figures, while the Chinese enemies are grotesque, cowering Asiatics with pigtails. It is as though the Japanese suddenly belonged to a different race, one akin to Europeans.

Most Japanese shared Fukuzawa's patriotic view of the war. Cutting China down to size meant Japan had joined the great nations. It also gave Japanese a new sense of national unity. The emperor had moved with his government to the war headquarters in Hiroshima, as an example of what Fukuzawa described as a "perfect cooperation between the government and the people." Newspapers reported the exploits of war heroes such as Shirakami Genjiro, the legendary bugler who kept on sounding the charge even after he had been shot through his lung. Current hit songs bore such titles as "The Dynamite Song" or "The Chinks."

Lafcadio Hearn, living in Japan at the time, wrote that the "real birthday of New Japan—began with the conquest of China." People felt that now, surely, the world—the Western world, that is—would take Japan seriously. A famous journalist wrote: "We are no longer ashamed to stand before the world as Japanese." This encapsulated the dark side of *Bunmei Kaika,* the idea that colonial conquest was the ultimate sign of greatness and modernity. It is where the other Meiji slogan, "Rich Country, Strong Army," kicked in.

Many, if not most, men of Meiji were heirs to such Edo intellectuals as Honda Toshiaki, who believed that no serious nation could be without an empire. The Sino-Japanese War was fought over supremacy in Korea, but its aims were wider than that. Even as he engaged in his dancing diplomacy, Foreign Minister Inoue Kaoru was keen to establish a Japanese empire in those parts of Asia that had not yet been taken by Western powers. The Japanese, as the great modernizers of Asia, set out to modernize the backward Koreans. When the Japanese took over Taiwan as a spoil of their victory, they vowed to make it into a model of enlightened colonialism. Japan, in the words of another flag-waving Japanese journalist, would finally be able to share with the Western powers in "this great and glorious work." What had not been achieved through cultural mimicry in ballrooms and fancy clubs had been brought about by blood and iron. Japan was now a power of substance. Just before the Japanese army defeated the forces of imperial China, the unequal treaties with the West ended. And now that they had proven their military mettle, Japan was able to inflict similarly unequal treaties on China. The lesson learned from Commodore Perry had finally borne its dark fruit.

———

National unity, the Darwinian struggle for national survival, racial vigor: These were themes that played all over the late-nineteenth-century world. Everywhere, new nations were being created and new national identities defined. More or less violent debates on these issues raged within nations, but there were certain distinctly national flavors. French reactionaries still pined for the ancien régime, but the republican idea of nationhood had struck roots in France; citizenship was defined by political rights, not by race or creed. The same applied to British citizenship, even though Her Majesty's subjects, unlike French citizens, owed allegiance to a monarchy that defended one faith. Germany, which became a unified state only in 1871, a mere three years after the Meiji Restoration, had problems defining its nationhood. Many Germans lived outside the national borders. The German states within wished to preserve their own identities. Like Meiji Japan, Wilhelminian Germany had to forge a centralized state out of old fiefdoms and feudal domains. What made a German feel German was something less political than cultural and ethnic, not citizenship so much as *Kultur,* music, poetry, and race; you belonged if your language was German and you were of German stock. Given the brittleness of German political institutions and the recent memories of revolution (in 1848), Bismarck and the Prussian monarchs were deeply suspicious of party politics. Party politicians, in their view, were "selfish," and liberals were potential traitors. National unity, under the Prussian kaisers, would be imposed by military discipline and cultural propaganda about national essence and the German spirit. National strength would be forged in iron and fed with blood.

The Meiji oligarchs, despite some opposition even in their own ranks, chose to go the German route. This was partly because the oligarchs had come of age as warriors, for whom the notion of political liberalism or republicanism was alien. They knew that a constitution and the semblance of political representation were necessary accoutrements of a modern state. But they struggled to solve a problem that many Muslim states are still facing today. They wanted to be modern and invoke ancient traditions at the same time. This was achieved by grafting German dogmas onto Japanese myths. They shared the same mixture of military discipline, mystical monarchism, and blood-and-soil propaganda about national essences. The most influential architect of the new national order was not Ito Hirobumi, despite his Bismarckian mannerisms, or a ballroom dancer like Inoue Kaoru, but Ito's old comrade in arms Yamagata Aritomo. He considered two things to be vital for national survival: military preparedness and education. And the kind of education he favored fostered loyalty, discipline, and obedience and squashed "selfish" individualism.

Like Ito, General Yamagata was born in Choshu, in 1839. His father was a samurai foot soldier. Again like Ito, he studied under Yoshida Shoin, the fierce nationalist who tried to get Commodore Perry to take him to America. Unlike the more affable Ito, however, Yamagata was a stern, unsmiling disciplinarian who left his mark on Japanese institutions as a military man, first as home affairs minister in the 1880s and twice as prime minister in the 1890s. He was the archetypical military bureaucrat, of whom there would be too many more.

To see Yamagata as a reactionary is to miss the point. He was not nostalgic for the days of the Edo *bakufu*. Indeed, he welcomed Japan's transformation into a great modern state. Nor was he against using Western ideas. Like his teacher Yoshida Shoin, he was eager to learn from other countries and spent a year traveling around Europe just after the restoration. He even hired German jurists to draft Japanese laws. But he was always aware of the consequences of opening the country to modern influences. Access to new ideas might easily "confuse" people and make them rebellious. Western influences should not be allowed to undermine traditional values. Yamagata was home minister when the People's Rights Movement was stirring up popular disobedience. He asked Ito, who was prime minister in the early 1880s, to introduce harsher legislation "to deal with political parties," for otherwise "the goal of preserving the independence of our imperial nation" would be impossible.

Yamagata got his way. Restrictive laws did tie down party politics. But his most important legacy was the role of the Imperial Armed Forces. The idea of a national army of conscripts was revolutionary in a country where carrying arms had been the privilege of a military caste. Not only had samurai been the only Japanese entitled to bear swords (and commit ritual suicide), but they had owed their loyalty to the lords of their domains, not to a central government. No wonder, then, that many ex-samurai resisted such a radical innovation. But not Yamagata, who was a modernist in this respect. From 1873, all able-bodied Japanese men had to serve three years in the army and four years in the reserves. For most of them, this was their first taste of Westernization. They wore Western-style uniforms, lived in Western-style barracks, and learned about Western military technology. Many also learned to read and write. And what they read was mostly nationalist propaganda. The armed forces, and not Fukuzawa's academy or free speech societies, were the conduit for modernity for most young men in Meiji Japan.

Even as modern technology and Western ways became familiar to millions of men, old samurai ethics spread their way through all classes of Meiji society. This was a deliberate policy. To Yamagata and other like-minded military men, the conscript army was not only essential to defend the country against foreign enemies, but the best way to unify the nation. National unity was armed unity. National education was military education. The samurai virtues were now applied nationally. Loyalty and obedience to the emperor, who was paraded around the country in military uniform, was the highest form of patriotism.

In 1882, the emperor handed down a Rescript for Soldiers and Sailors, drafted by Yamagata. It was one of the most influential documents in modern Japanese history. The rescript spelled out the duties that every Japanese soldier and sailor had to learn by rote. Absolute loyalty was due only to the emperor: "We are your supreme Commander-in-Chief. Our relations with you will be most intimate when We rely on you as Our limbs and you look up to Us as your head." The emperor's troops were to refrain from politics. They were not to question imperial policies or even voice private opinions about them. Yamagata's aim was to remove the armed forces from politics, to lift them to a higher sphere where the only thing that mattered was the imperial will. He thought this would prevent rebellions. The flaw in this scheme would become obvious half a century later. For it often had the opposite effect. If a soldier's only duty was to the divine monarch, then it surely was legitimate to rebel against civilian leaders who were thought to ignore the imperial will. This was precisely what the sincerely fascistic young army officers thought in 1936, when they went around murdering cabinet ministers to show their loyalty to the throne.

Emperor worship, one of the pillars of Yamagata's new order, was presented as an ancient duty, as something inherent to the Japanese psyche, as the essence of Japanese

Kultur reaching back to the birth of the first Shinto gods. In fact this was as phony as the Gothic inventions in Wilhelminian Germany. Like German romantic medievalism, it borrowed elements from the past, to be sure, but the emperor cult that evolved in the Meiji era was as modern as Yamagata's conscript army. Japanese had never actually worshiped the emperor as the supreme deity before. Until the last years of the Edo period, he had lived in Kyoto, cultivating the arts, as a spiritual guardian of Japanese customs and morals. Shinto was not a state religion or cult, but a loose collection of animist rituals and seasonal feasts, celebrating nature, fertility, and gods who gave birth to Japan. In the Meiji period, however, Shinto gradually became state Shinto, a very different thing. What Yamagata and other Meiji oligarchs did was to politicize culture and religion, while neutralizing secular political institutions. Nationhood, despite the constitution, was based not on political rights, but on religious worship of the imperial institution and, through state Shinto, the idea of Japan itself.

The Imperial Rescript on Education, handed down in 1890, when Yamagata was still prime minister, told the Japanese people to be obedient to the emperor and his divine ancestors. In loyalty and filial piety, it said, lay the "glory of the fundamental character of Our Empire" and the "source of Our education." This was a reaction to the kind of Westernization promoted by such people as Fukuzawa Yukichi. Conservatives were convinced that the process of Westernization had gone too far and threatened the moral standards of the empire.

The notion was in fact profoundly Confucian. Despite all their kicking against Chinese influences and all their mystical talk of deep Japaneseness, Japanese authorities were still steeped in neo-Confucian ways of thinking. The idea that common people are to be controlled through moral exhortation and enforced intellectual conformity is Chinese in origin. Constitutionally, there may have been freedom of religion in Japan, but in fact there was little room for dissent, for the source of power remained the source of truth. Aside from the Buddhists, Japanese Christians got the full blast of nativist propaganda. They were tolerated at first. Some of the most famous Meiji intellectuals were Christians. But after the rescript, life became increasingly difficult, for you could not worship two gods. If Japanese Christians wanted to be assimilated to the national polity of Japan, opined a well-known Meiji professor, Christianity would have to be completely destroyed, for sovereignty in Japan was vested in a single "race-father."

The idea of an imperial God who was also commander in chief of the armed forces was already a radical departure from Japanese tradition. The idea that he was a race-father—indeed, the very thought of a national "race"—smacked of modern German-style ethnic nationalism, mixed up with nativist doctrines of the mid-nineteenth-century Mito School. It would be quite wrong, then, to see Yamagata's authoritarian reaction to "Civilization and Enlightenment" as a break with modernity or Westernization. He, too, had borrowed ideas from the West. They just happened to be highly illiberal ones. The type of Japanese to emerge from his kind of education was far from Fukuzawa's ideal. Instead of skeptical individualists, Japanese military training, in schools as well as the barracks, was bent on creating well-drilled conformists, singularly ill equipped to think for themselves.

—

The high point of Meiji militarism was the brutal war against Russia, which began with a Pearl Harbor–type raid on the Russian fleet in 1904. The Japanese were still feeling bruised because Western powers forced them to hand over some of their victory spoils in 1895. This included the southern tip of the Liaotung peninsula in Manchuria, which was then leased to the Russians. Western powers were feasting on Chinese territory just then: Germans in Shandong, the French in Canton, the British in various treaty ports along the coast. The Americans were expanding their Asian empire in the Pacific. The Russians acquired railway concessions in Manchuria and were moving into north Korea, which Japan saw as its turf. So the Japanese had ample reason to feel left out of the party.

The only consolation for Japan was its alliance with Britain in 1902. The German kaiser, Wilhelm II, loathed the Japanese despite their Germanophilia, and he frequently warned the czar of the "yellow peril." The Russians brushed off Japanese attempts to discuss their respective interests in northeast Asia. So the Japanese navy, under Admiral Togo Heihachiro, struck hard, first at Port Arthur and later in the Tsushima Strait, after which there was nothing much left of Russia's mighty Baltic fleet. Like the Americans some four decades later, the Russians were utterly unprepared. They never thought the Japanese would dare attack a major Western power. Such a thing was unheard of, at least since the days of Genghis Khan. The British press, on the other hand, was full of admiration for the "plucky little Japs."

After one year of war, hundreds of thousands of Japanese and Russians had died in some of the most savage battles ever seen. The Russo-Japanese War was a kind of dress rehearsal for World War I. Gone were the brave buglers and colorful banners of the Sino-Japanese conflict. This time, two great armies slaughtered each other from barbed-wired trenches. To gain a few yards in muddy, rain-soaked terrain, thousands of men staggered into mine fields and machine-gun fire. In the battle for Port Arthur, General Nogi Maresuke's army suffered fifty-eight thousand casualties, dead and wounded. One of the dead was his son. But Nogi, the paragon of Meiji patriotism, claimed this filled him with nothing but pride. At Mukden, the Russians suffered eighty-five thousand casualties and the Japanese seventy thousand. But after all that, Japan did get the Manchurian railway rights and the lease of the Liaotung peninsula. One of the foreign observers in this ghastly conflict was a young American lieutenant named Douglas MacArthur.

The victory mood in Tokyo was no longer as festive as in 1895, perhaps because too many people had died. The war songs were melancholy more than triumphant. The state had only just been saved from bankruptcy when Jacob Schiff, a Jewish banker in New York who was outraged by Russian pogroms, decided to come to Japan's rescue. This strengthened Japanese credulity when captured Russian officers introduced them to anti-Semitic tracts about the supposed omnipotence of the Elders of Zion. Schiff, it seemed clear, was one of the Jews who secretly ruled the world: yet another wrong lesson picked up from the West. In some instances, the mood in Japan turned positively ugly. Enraged nationalists, but also members of the People's Rights Movement, rioted in Tokyo because Russia had not been pressed to pay war reparations. A new generation, fed less on the idealism of the early restoration than on the hysterical chauvinism of the latter, more belli- cose period, began to make itself felt. The oligarchs were passing from the scene. Yamagata, who had always been in favor of fostering a military but not a militant spirit, wor- ried that future conflicts would be race wars between West and East.

———

Natsume Soseki, the most brilliant novelist of his time, warned darkly that Japan had tried to digest Western civi- lization too quickly and was heading for a collective nervous breakdown. With Fukuzawa Yukichi, Soseki rep- resented the best of Meiji. A man of real civilization and enlightenment, he exhibited a knowledge of Chinese, Japa- nese, and European literary culture that was rare in his time and almost unheard of today. Soseki was a humane, independent-minded, tortured writer. *Kokoro,* perhaps his finest novel, reflects all these qualities. It is the story of a relationship between a student and an older intellectual, known to his pupil simply as *sensei,* "Master." They belong to different generations, master and pupil, divided by growing up in different times, different worlds. Master is tormented by a sense of guilt over his role in the youth- ful suicide of his best friend. He suffers also from a sense of isolation, of being an anachronism. When the Meiji em- peror dies in the summer of 1912, he feels that his age has passed. He reads in the paper that General Nogi, hero of the Russo-Japanese War, committed suicide on the day of his emperor's death. To die in this manner for one's lord was already an anachronism a century before. Master, too, decides to kill himself.

General Nogi Maresuke, despite the old-fashioned style

of his death, was as typical of his age as Fukuzawa, Ito, Yamagata, or Natsume Soseki. Like Soseki's Master, he harbored feelings of guilt. Commanding government troops in the war against Saigo Takamori's samurai in the Satsuma rebellion of 1877, Nogi lost his regimental flag and thought of committing suicide then to atone for this disgrace. But he lived on to fight in the Sino-Japanese War and, of course, as a legendary general in the war against the Russians. He lost both his sons in the latter conflict. Grief did not deflect him from his purpose. After the death of his second son, he said he would consider it an honor to die for the emperor.

And in a manner of speaking he did, out of patriotism, but also, possibly, out of guilt for losing his sons. On the day of his emperor's funeral, Nogi wrote a short poem about Mount Fuji and his wish for Japan to be united in memory of the heroes who died for the emperor. His wife changed into a black kimono, and Nogi stripped to his white undergarments. After bowing to portraits of the late emperor and of their two sons, General Nogi let his wife die first by plunging a dagger into her neck, then died the samurai's death by cutting his stomach with a short sword. It was, as I said, a quaint way to go even then. But General Nogi and his wife, as models of ideal behavior, set the tone for future years, at least as much as Fukuzawa and his more liberal ways, and possibly more. Few could ever wish to live up to their example, but enough would try, with often grotesque and ultimately catastrophic results.

Every ten-thousand-yen bill has a portrait of Fukuzawa, and Natsume Soseki is on the one-thousand-yen notes. General Nogi might have been horrified had he been remembered in such a pecuniary way. But he has not been forgotten, even now. His house in Tokyo can still be seen, next to a shrine dedicated to the general's soul. Twice a year, on the eve and anniversary of his death, the public is invited to walk around the house on an elevated path, and if you look carefully through one of the windows, you can just make out the bloodstained undershirt of the man people called the Last Samurai.

3

ERO GURO NANSENSU

The year 1920 was, for many Japanese, the best of times. World War I, fought by others on the far side of the world, had come as a stroke of luck. While European powers wasted their resources and millions of young men on war, the Japanese built ships, exported textiles, made industrial machines and railway rolling stock, and supplied the Europeans with munitions. By the end of the war, the Japanese economy was booming, with large combines such as Mitsubishi and Sumitomo at the top and countless small workshops at the bottom of the industrial pile. As an added bonus, Japan was able to secure some spoils for itself. Having joined the Allies, Japan expanded its empire by grabbing German possessions in China and the South Pacific.

The oppressive air that had hung over the last Meiji years had lifted. The Taisho emperor, Yoshihito, a feeble-witted man, inspired none of the awe enjoyed by his father, even as a symbolic figure. Once, when the poor man was asked to grace the Diet with his presence, he allegedly rolled up a document and used it as a telescope. He was rarely seen in public again. (His son, Hirohito, had to step in as regent in 1922.) The old Meiji patriarchs had died or were too old to assert their authority. And for the first time, the prime minister of Japan was not an old bureaucrat but a party politician.

There was some trouble in the Japanese empire, to be sure. In March 1919, Koreans rebelled against their forced assimilation as second-class Japanese subjects. A Japanese protectorate since the Russo-Japanese War in 1905, Korea had been annexed by Japan in 1910. Some members of the Korean elite welcomed this and collaborated with the Japanese, but most Koreans, especially university students, hated being bossed around by officials from a nation whose culture they considered less civilized than their own. Thousands gathered in Pagoda Park in the center of Seoul and declared independence. Up to half a million Koreans from all walks of life came out in support. The Japanese gendarmerie, armed with sabers and rifles, charged. The rebellion was crushed, but the massacre of at least seven thousand protesters, many of them students, was so shocking that even the Japanese government acknowledged that something had gone badly wrong.

The Chinese May 4th Movement in that same year, protesting the Japanese takeover of the German concessions in China, was as hostile to Japan as it was toward the abject Chinese government. And there had been trouble at home as well. Inflation and a short slump after the war caused poverty in the countryside and high unemployment. In August 1918, rioters all over Japan burned down police stations, shops, rich people's houses, and, oddly, a few expensive brothels in Tokyo, in protest against the high price of rice. Still, it was a hopeful sign that Japanese felt free to openly criticize their government. The early 1920s was above all a time of movements: for universal suffrage, for the liberation of discriminated outcasts, and for women's rights. On the whole, then, it was a good time to be young.

———

The Ginza in Tokyo, that Europeanized center of "Civilization and Enlightenment," had changed a great deal since the dark days of late Meiji. Longhaired young men in *roido* (from Harold Lloyd) glasses, bell-bottom trousers, colored shirts, and floppy ties would stroll down the willow-lined avenue with young women in bobbed hairdos. The more earnest ones, who gathered in "milk bars" to discuss German philosophy or Russian novels, were known as Marx boys and Marx girls. A few years later, the fashionable young would be renamed *mobos* (modern boys) and their flapper girlfriends *mogas* (modern girls). Aside from the milk bars, the Ginza abounded in German-style beer halls and Parisian-style cafés, with waitresses who were free with their favors—for a modest fee. Many patrons of these establishments, with such names as Tiger Café and Lion Beer Hall, were journalists, who, like the café waitresses, were a feature of this bright new age of mass media and entertainment. Up the street, near Hibiya Park, where the riots of 1905 took place, Frank Lloyd Wright was building the Imperial Hotel, where people would take their tea and eat ultrafashionable "Chaplin caramels."

A tram ride to the east of the Ginza took one to Asakusa, the center of popular entertainment. This is where the latest Hollywood movies were shown in art deco cinemas and lines of half-naked chorus girls kicked up their legs at the "opera." In 1920, one might have seen *The Lasciviousness of the Viper,* directed by "Thomas" Kurihara, who had learned his craft in Hollywood. So had another director of silent movies, "Frank" Tokunaga, who insisted on speaking English to his Japanese crews, putting his studio to the unnecessary expense of having to provide an interpreter. There were posters everywhere advertising swordfight movies about Sakamoto Ryoma and other Edo swashbucklers. There were cabaret shows, comic storytellers, Western, Chinese, and Japanese restaurants. And there was some real opera, too. An Italian from Britain had introduced Tokyoites to the delights of Verdi.

Taisho Tokyo was marked by a skittish, sometimes nihilistic hedonism that brings Weimar Berlin to mind. It produced a culture that would later be summed up as *ero* for erotic, *guro* for grotesque, and *nansensu,* which speaks for itself. In some instances, the similarities with Berlin were more than coincidental. Painters and cartoonists did pictures à la George Grosz. Directors of the New Theater put on plays by Hauptmann and Maeterlinck and studied Max Reinhardt and Stanislavsky. Dada, expressionism, cubism, constructivism, new sobriety: All had had their day in Japan—more than a day, in fact, since trends tend to stick around a lot longer there than in their countries of origin. Novelists looked to Europe, too. Tanizaki Junichiro adopted the style of fin-de-siècle French decadents. One of the best movies of the period, Kinugasa Teinosuke's *Page of Madness,* owed much to *The Cabinet of Dr. Caligari.* He made this film only a few years after appearing himself in another, far more conventional picture, playing a woman in a kimono and a pair of sturdy rain boots to cope with the open-air location—theatrical realism was late in coming, even in the movies. Taisho was a time of radical politics, but also of artistic experimentation and introspection. Individualism was carried to the point of self-obsession. Literary diaries recording every nuance of the author's moods, known as "I-novels," were highly popular. Far removed from the earnest idealism of Meiji, artists were keen to explore the limits of romantic love and dark eroticism.

Students at elite institutions were just as eager for new ideas. They cultivated a Sakamoto Ryoma–like slovenliness in their dress, used words like "lumpen proletariat" and "bourgeois liberalism" a great deal, and took a passionate interest in DeKanSho, short for Descartes, Kant, and Schopenhauer. Intellectual young women from wealthy families insisted on learning more than household skills, and in 1918 the first women's university was established in

Tokyo. Even soldiers were brushed by the fresh winds of early Taisho. The army minister, Tanaka Giichi, worried that his troops had "become bold and rebellious in their attitudes," and one commander complained that "due to the rise in general knowledge and social education," his men could no longer be counted on to follow orders blindly.

———

So what went wrong? Why had this freewheeling Japanese Weimar spirit been brought down—though not out—by about 1932? For an answer, we would have to look at the power of the imperial court and the military establishment, but also at the nature of political rebellion in Japan. The problem was visible already in 1905, when riots broke out against the Portsmouth Treaty, which concluded the Russo-Japanese War. On first sight, the protest was pure jingoism. The newspapers were particularly violent in their opposition to a treaty that, in editorial opinions, was too soft on the Russians. But the crowds that gathered in Hibiya Park on September 5, after having stormed the police barriers and the few policemen who got in their way, were even fiercer. "The war must go on!" they yelled as brass bands played military marches. People sang the national anthem, cheered for the emperor and his army, and marched to the imperial palace, where they clashed with the police.

The riots in Tokyo went on for several days. There were up to a thousand casualties. Thirteen Christian churches were wrecked and looted, one of them in Asakusa, where the priest had been unwise enough to preach that Russia had got favorable terms because it was a Christian country. Government buildings and police boxes lay in ruins. For some time, the capital looked out of control. Yet there was more to this than chauvinism. For the leaders of the riots were not all right-wing zealots, but included veterans of the People's Rights Movement and advocates of universal suffrage. One of them had sent a telegram to the army in Manchuria, urging it to crush the enemy, and petitioned the Privy Council to tear up the treaty.

The Japanese rioters, in fact, behaved very much like their Chinese counterparts in 1919, who protested against *their* government for letting Japan take over the German concessions. When governments rule without popular representation or even consent, one form of rebellion is to be more nationalistic than the rulers. If the rulers are traitors to the nation, they should be overthrown. It is a pattern that has occurred over and over again in east Asia, and it is not very conducive to liberal democracy. It also shows that demands for political rights at home can exist quite happily with imperialist demands abroad. But this is a game that both sides can play; the authorities can turn nationalist sentiments against the liberals, too, and frequently did.

Still, in the early Taisho period it looked as if parliamentary democracy might yet have a chance. The rice riots of 1918 laid the groundwork for the first government formed by a member of the lower house, an elected party politician named Hara Kei. The riots were about more than rice, of course, just as the protests against the Portsmouth Treaty went beyond demands for further Russian concessions. They were an opportunity for all those who felt left behind by the new industrial age to vent their frustration: construction workers, rickshaw drivers, farmers, and small shopkeepers, as well as members of the *burakumin,* or outcast communities, who had been emancipated legally in 1900 but still faced discrimination. By blaming the outcasts for the violence, the authorities tried to manipulate popular prejudices. It didn't work. Instead, the discredited prime minister, General Terauchi, had to resign.

Hara Kei was a skillful politician who had to find a way of juggling the interests of his own party, the Seiyukai, and those of the institutions that held the real power in Japanese politics: the House of Peers, stacked with retired military men, old courtiers, and conservative bureaucrats; the emperor's advisory body, otherwise known as the Privy Council, which decided the most important matters of state; and the army and navy ministers, who had to be serving military officers. While the oligarchs were still active, they managed these various groups as if they were the board members of a very grand gentlemen's club. The authority of men such as Yamagata Aritomo and Ito Hirobumi was enough to make it work. Frictions were smoothed, faces saved, feathers unruffled, protégés pushed, and interests reconciled through discreet meetings and gentlemen's agreements. And all this behind the veil of the imperial will. After the oligarchs left the scene, however, through death or old age, Japanese politics became a constant battle between institutions, without anyone to preside. The imperial will, especially under the Taisho emperor but also under his son, Hirohito, really was no more than a screen around a snakepit.

Hara's way of expanding the power of parliament, and thus of party politics, was by playing the same game that kept the conservative Liberal Democratic Party in office more or less continuously since the 1950s. Already as home minister in previous governments, he had cultivated local landowners, businessmen, and industrialists by setting up a network of rich pork barrels: railways here, bridges, roads, and new factories there. Sweet deals and kickbacks made it worth the while of bureaucrats to be involved in Hara's party machine. It worked, up to a point. But when Hara became prime minister, criticisms of official corruption met with harsh crackdowns. Special thought police, established in 1911, went after writers and publishers of "dangerous" books. "Dangerous" was, of course, a flexible concept, but any kind of socialism would normally fall under its rubric.

Hara was by no means a radical. He did little to promote universal male suffrage. The reason he became prime minister in the first place was his careful cultivation of Yamagata while the old oligarch was still powerful. Even so, he was too radical for some. Hara upset senior figures in the navy by agreeing to sign a treaty with the United States, Britain, and France and limiting the buildup of Japan's battle fleet. So it was no surprise, really, that Hara was assassinated in 1921 by another of those sincere zealots who did so much to wreck the chances of Japanese democracy.

As was true in most Western countries, democracy was still a relative term even among Japanese liberals. One of the great activists for universal male suffrage and constitutional government was Yoshino Sakuzo, a graduate of the Tokyo Imperial University law faculty. This august institution was the academic nursery for the bureaucratic elite. Renamed Tokyo University after the war, it still is. Yoshino could have joined the select and secretive band of men who administered Japan in the emperor's name. Instead, like Fukuzawa Yukichi a generation before, he chose that most precious, precarious, and indeed dangerous of occupations: to be an independent intellectual. Like many east Asian liberal activists, he was also a Christian convert.

In 1905, a year after his graduation, Yoshino began to publish his critical views of autocratic government and "militaristic imperialism." Although he did not believe Japan was ready for American-style democracy, he liked to quote Lincoln's Gettysburg Address. The only way to compete as a serious power, he argued, was to have a constitutional government and what he called "people-centered democracy." Unlike some Christians, he had been totally in favor of the war against Russia, since Russia, in his view, was a feudal dictatorship and Japan the natural master of Korea and Manchuria. But since people were asked to fight—and thus often to die—for their country, they should surely have a voice in the way they were governed. This formed the basis of what came to be known, to those who looked back fondly, or with loathing, as "Taisho democracy."

Yoshino was a liberal-minded reformist, the kind who so often got trampled on in Japanese politics. He was a socialist, but not a revolutionary—a distinction that was often lost on Japanese authorities. One day, he thought, the mystique of the imperial institution would fade, but not yet. One day, the Koreans might have real autonomy, but not absolute independence. One day, the Chinese, Koreans, and Japanese would come together in opposition to militarism and capitalist exploitation. He wanted to limit the almost unlimited authority of the Privy Council and if possible do away with it altogether. Yoshino was about as democratic as it was possible to be at the time. But he was not a leader of violent demonstrations, which were still the only way for common people to voice their discontent.

Instead, Yoshino wrote for liberal journals, gave lectures, taught at Tokyo Imperial University, studied abroad, worked as a journalist for the *Asahi* newspaper, and, in the tradition of the early Meiji debating clubs, started the Shinjinkai, an informal society for clever "Marx boys" to discuss social and political affairs. He had spent some time in China as a teacher and wrote positive articles in the

Japanese press about the May 4th Movement in 1919. He also visited Korea in 1916, where he saw the brutality of Japanese authorities and the futility of their efforts to turn Koreans into Japanese. The official propaganda about Koreans being of the same race and culture as the Japanese was fatally undermined by official and unofficial discrimination. He told his Japanese readers that to be Korean was to be anti-Japanese, a fact, alas, that still holds true for many Koreans almost a hundred years later. The 1919 rebellion, Yoshino held, was "a stain on the Taisho period." Such an uprising had to be put down, of course, but he strongly argued for fairer treatment of the Koreans. A staunch imperialist, then, but a humane one. The limitation of Taisho liberalism—as much as its nobility—was reflected in Yoshino's thinking. If even a liberal such as Yoshino could find no principal objection to Japanese domination of its neighbors, it becomes easier to understand how Japan could later embark on far more perilous military adventures.

One of the worst instances of Japanese brutality toward Koreans came in the aftermath of the earthquake that devastated Tokyo and Yokohama in 1923. The whole city began to lurch violently around lunchtime. Within hours, much of Tokyo was burning. Wild rumors spread as swiftly as the fires: Foreigners had attacked Japan with an earthquake machine; Koreans had gone around poisoning the wells. There was nothing much people could do against "foreigners," since there were comparatively few, but mobs did go around killing Koreans, drowning them in the Sumida River or beating and trampling them to death amid the smoldering ruins. One person who tried to protect them was Yoshino Sakuzo. He also did his best to revise the low official estimates of the Korean death toll and arrived at a figure near two thousand.

In 1923 there was still hope for those who promoted freedom. Two years later, the government led by Kato Takaaki, a wealthy Anglophile who emulated the upper-class British manner, managed at last to pass a law giving the vote to all men over twenty-five with a steady income. Considering where Japan was a mere century before, and where the rest of Asia still was at that time, this was a stupendous achievement. But it was also as if a step forward had to be immediately countered by a reverse. A week later, the Peace Preservation Law made it illegal to participate in any organized opposition to the *kokutai,* or national polity. This meant that communists or radical socialists could face up to ten years in jail.

Kato died a year later, remarkably, of natural causes. Following a brief interlude under the stewardship of a general, the government fell to an even more interesting politician, Hamaguchi Osachi, leader of the Progressive Party, or Minseito. He had great plans to give women the vote in local elections, reform labor-management relations, and improve relations with China. In London in 1930, he agreed to sign a naval treaty that put further limits on a Japanese naval buildup. And then things went badly wrong. The navy chief of staff was enraged by what he saw as a politician encroaching on his turf, since this was a naval affair and thus, in his view, outside civilian control. Hamaguchi was shot by a right-wing fanatic at the Tokyo railway station and died a few weeks later. Litle more than a year after that, Prime Minister Inukai Tsuyoshi, who was trying desperately to keep radical army and navy factions from going to war with China, was murdered by a group of naval officers, called the Blood Pledge Society, in an attempted coup d'état. Two business leaders were killed as well, while other fanatics were bombing such symbols of right-wing hate as Inukai's party offices and the Bank of Japan. By then, the experiment with party government was over. Manchuria had been turned into a puppet state. And the war in China was only just beginning.

—

The Weimar Republic was destroyed by Hitler not only through the brutality of his storm troopers, but also because too few people were prepared to defend its fragile institutions. Communists and social democrats were too busy fighting each other to fully appreciate the seriousness of the Nazi threat. Taisho democracy, too, never had enough defenders. Already in 1916, Yoshino Sakuzo, the liberal thinker, wrote that many Japanese intellectuals failed to see the point of universal suffrage. Indeed, many loathed it. Like so many disillusioned German intellectuals, they saw democratic politics as vulgar, debased, selfish, and corrupt. This led to radical antiliberalism on the one hand and morbid introspection on the other. One was sometimes the result of the other.

The most influential Japanese philosopher of the early twentieth century was Nishida Kitaro. Deeply immersed in German idealism as well as Buddhist thought, Nishida tried to articulate a new, uniquely Japanese way of thinking. Seeking the essence of Japaneseness was the Japanese version of German idealism. It emerged, like so many products of early modern Japan, as a hybrid in which Zen got mixed up with Hegel, Nietzsche, and, especially in the hands of Nishida's acolytes, Heidegger. The basis of Nishida's thought was the fusion of subject and object. What was needed was direct experience, unhampered by reason, a kind of melding of Buddhist satori, or instinctive enlightenment, and Hegel's "absolute Spirit," where the individual is dissolved in the collective. This kind of thing would have been harmless had it been confined to the halls of Kyoto Imperial University. But it was not. A notorious tract published in 1937 by the Ministry of Education, entitled *Kokutai no Hongi* (*Fundamentals of the National Polity*), told Japanese to "abandon" their "small egos" and "seek in the emperor" the source of their existence. The Japanese, in the purity of their spirit, were superior to all other nations and "completely different in [their] nature from the so-called citizens of Western nations." This politically toxic document was a vulgarized version of Nishida's view of the Japanese subject dissolved in the imperial object.

The careers of two men, both born in 1883, show how such devotion could come as a welcome relief to Taisho-period figures who had tried hard to be individualists. The first was Kita Ikki. He began his intellectual journey as a romantic devotee of Nietzsche and Nichiren Buddhism. In the overheated atmosphere of 1920s Japan, Nichiren spawned a school of belief that held that imperial Japan would one day be the center of a unified world, but only after Jews and democrats were defeated. There were obvious traces here of borrowed Russian propaganda; Jews were largely unheard of in Japan.

Kita's family background was neither xenophobic nor particularly romantic. He was the son of a sake merchant on the remote island of Sado. His father was a firm supporter of the People's Rights Movement. From an early age, Kita was seized by the ideal of absolute individual freedom. But the question of people's rights was too tame for him. In fact, he wasn't interested in peaceful politics at all. He was after absolutes and violent acts of will. As it did many Japanese idealists of his age, individualism confused him. Inspired by his beloved Nietzsche, he began searching for ways to overcome his sense of individual isolation by fusing the human and the divine. In 1911, he witnessed the revolution in China, which brought down the Qing dynasty, and was so excited that he adopted a Chinese name. His thoughts soon turned to a Japanese revolution.

Revolutionary violence, for Kita, was not so much political as religious, an act of personal, spiritual liberation. He made contacts with members of extreme right-wing groups and wrote political pamphlets that promoted a kind of national socialism with the emperor as the religious führer. The state, he argued, had been hijacked by corrupt oligarchs, bureaucrats, bankers, and industrialists. The oligarchs had tricked the Japanese people by limiting the emperor's political power through the vaguely worded Meiji constitution. What was needed was a coup d'état that would give the "people's emperor" absolute power. The individual would be liberated by total identification with the emperor and the nation. The nation was an organism, a "large self," as he put it, that would absorb the "small selves" of all individual subjects. And beyond the imperial nation lay nirvana, where the self would become God. Kita Ikki had come a long way from his father's liberalism. But he had a sacred cause for which to live or, what is more important, to die.

Kita's cause had a particular appeal to junior officers in the army, who were mostly from poor rural areas and, like Kita Ikki, blamed capitalist city slickers for the corruption and degradation of the nation. A number of these men, burning with violent idealism, staged a coup in February 1936, aiming to give absolute power to the emperor and purge the *kokutai* of traitors and corrupt officials. The coup was crushed, and Kita was arrested as the man behind the scenes. If the coup had succeeded, he would have been made minister without portfolio. He was executed together with sixteen others.

Kita Ikki's story shows how combustible Japanese society had become in his lifetime. He was not just an oddball, operating in the rancid margins of right-wing extremism. From the early 1920s, he had regular meetings with Admiral Togo Heihachiro, hero of the Russo-Japanese War and still an influential player in navy politics. Kita's brand of mystical chauvinism was both revolutionary and dangerously close to the ambitions of far more powerful enemies of democracy. Just two years after Kita's execution, Araki Sadao, the education minister, wrote that the Japanese empire, subject to divine will, "rests upon the foundation of blood relationship, which far transcends mere morality, and our Ruler is viewed in the light of a super-moral Being. . . ." Note the "mere" morality; it could have been written by Kita himself.

Takamura Kotaro's career was not violent like Kita Ikki's, nor did he have any significant political influence. He was a sculptor and a poet. But his life demonstrated, perhaps even more clearly than Kita's, how difficult it was to be an individualist in early modern Japan. His attitudes to the West, and to his own country, were an extreme version of what many Japanese intellectuals went through at the time.

The son of a well-known sculptor, Takamura had a deep interest in European art. Rodin was a particular passion. After studying Western art in Tokyo, he went to New York in 1906 and began to write poetry, then moved to London, where he met the potter Bernard Leach, and finally, in 1908, traveled to Paris, the city of his beloved

Rodin and Baudelaire. Back in Tokyo the following year, he lived the life of a Westernized bohemian, loathing the provincial stuffiness of Meiji Japan, always comparing it unfavorably to cosmopolitan Paris. In one poem, entitled "The Japanese," he rehearsed everything he hated about his fellow countrymen, those "Monkey-like, foxlike, squirrel-like, gudgeon-like, minnow-like, potsherd-like, gargoyle-faced Japanese!"

This was in 1911, when Takamura's memories of his years in the West were still relatively happy. He said he had felt completely relaxed in Paris. He had even been able to forget his nationality there, which is something for a Japanese. Perhaps, however, he found it hard to live as a Parisian-style bohemian in Tokyo. He might have felt isolated in his own society. Whatever the reason, in the 1920s a different tone crept into Takamura's poems, a peevish sense of alienation sometimes bordering on hysteria. His European years were now remembered as a time of loneliness and rejection. An episode with a Frenchwoman was recalled with bitterness. The morning after his erotic encounter, he saw himself in the mirror as a "Mongol," as *le Jaune*, the yellow Jap. Self-hatred gradually curdled into xenophobia and racial chauvinism. In the 1930s, he wrote poems celebrating the glories of Japanese militarism. It was as if, with the onset of war, he could turn with relief to such phrases as "my country, Japan," or "we Japanese." In a poem addressed to Chiang Kai-shek, he wrote:

> My country, Japan, is not destroying yours, sir;
> We're only destroying anti-Japanese thought.

He was released at last from the strain of being a Westernized individualist.

It was sentiments such as these, widely shared by Japanese intellectuals, that made it so hard to resist the propaganda of national unity and emperor worship. Communists and some radical socialists held out, and critical journalism continued to appear, despite the censors' efforts, but as time went on, liberals were squeezed between the hard Left and the violent Right. And the mainstream political parties, such as Hara Kei's Seiyukai or Hamaguchi's Minseito, did nothing to help the liberals. In the late 1920s, the lower house voted for laws that suppressed political dissent, and the party politicians supported police crackdowns not only on the radical Left, but on many social democrats, too. Their ultimately futile attempt to protect the authority of the parliament led them to pander to the chauvinism of their enemies in the bureaucracy, the imperial court, and the armed forces. In the end, as always happens in such circumstances, they ended up being crushed themselves.

———

Even as Admiral Togo Heihachiro was taking a keen interest in Kita Ikki's revolutionary theories, he was invested with the task of grooming the next emperor. Crown Prince Hirohito's first and possibly most influential teacher had been General Nogi, the other hero of the Russo-Japanese War. After Nogi slit his stomach out of loyalty to the Meiji emperor, Hirohito's grandfather, Admiral Togo took over the supervision of the young prince's education. More or less totally cloistered from the outside world, Hirohito was drilled in such military pursuits as shooting, map reading, strategy, and horse riding. A small, sensitive, inarticulate boy, he was hardly a martial type by nature, but he did his best.

Hirohito's young mind was also filled with all kinds of odd notions, which owed as much to the late-nineteenth-century nativism of the Mito School as to the latest Germanic race theories. He was taught the myths of Japanese racial purity and the divine provenance of his own bloodlines as though these were historical facts. Much was made of the Darwinian struggle of the Japanese race with the "Aryan" nations. Above all, he was continually warned against the "poison of European liberal thought." His teachers were extremely worried that democratic ideas would undermine the awesome authority of the imperial institution, the preservation of which was the monarch's highest duty. The fall of European monarchies in 1918 had come as a shock. Kaiser Wilhelm II's defeat was held up as a cautionary tale. In effect, Hirohito's education was a form of counterpropaganda against the struggling Taisho democracy.

This is not to say that he was told to be on the side of right-wing extremists. Order was the main thing, and national unity. But when Hirohito expressed his fear of "extremist thought," which he did on various occasions, the type of thing he had in mind was not Kita Ikki or other right-wingers, but Marxism, social democracy, or even democracy *tout court*. Social harmony, and thus the preservation of order, had to be based on a shared consciousness of racial homogeneity, on military discipline and reverence for the emperor. Anything else was disruptive and divisive and would lead to selfishness and chaos.

Hirohito became regent in 1922, when his unfortunate father was removed from the scene. But just before that, Hirohito had his first and only taste of a kind of freedom. In 1921, it was deemed a necessary step in his education to send the crown prince on a trip to Europe. Some conservatives were opposed to this, since exposure to foreign ways would pollute his pure and august status. Others worried that this awkward youth would make Japan look less than superior in foreign eyes. But off he went, via Hong Kong, Singapore, and Ceylon, to Britain, France, Holland, and Italy. He learned much that was new to him: the fact that people carried money to pay for things like public transport, for example. He was impressed by the informality of British aristocratic manners, even at Buckingham Palace. It must have been astonishing to see people at a royal court behave like relatively normal human beings. Struck by the warm relations between the duke of Atholl and his tenants, Hirohito stated that with such politics, there would be "no need to worry about extremist thought." He tried to emulate the British style after he got back home. Apart from a lifelong penchant for fried eggs and bacon, the practice was, however, swiftly discontinued.

The Taisho emperor died in 1926. The enthronement of his son was staged as a huge media event. Day and night, newspapers and radio broadcasts reported rice-growing ceremonies, flag-waving parades, lantern festivals, award ceremonies, and Shinto rituals of various kinds, some of which had been quite recently invented. Many books were written, and lectures delivered, on the essence of Japanese-ness and the *kokutai,* and many warnings were given about the dangers of dissent. Reverence for ancestors, unity of the monarch and the people, and the unity of rites and governance were presented by learned men not just as Japanese, but as "scientific" principles. The Peace Preservation Law, first promulgated in 1925, was revised to expand the powers of the thought police, who redoubled their efforts to root out radicals in universities, newspapers, publishing houses, or wherever they might be. The armed forces established their own thought police to protect the *kokutai.*

The climax of all this came on November 14, 1928, or rather on the following morning, when Emperor Hirohito was formally reborn as a living god, after having spent the night in the holiest of holy shrines at Ise, communing with his progenitor, sun goddess Amaterasu Omikami. Two weeks later, the new emperor was in Tokyo, dressed in military uniform, watching impassively as more than thirty-five thousand troops came marching by. This was followed by a review of the imperial fleet, including 2 aircraft carriers, 208 ships, and 39 submarines. Millions who turned on the radio that day, in Japan, Taiwan, Korea, or wherever the rising-sun flag was raised, could hear the sounds of marching boots, gun salutes, and navy aircraft flying low. The period named Showa, "illustrious peace," had begun.

4

AH, OUR MANCHURIA

S o when did the Japanese war begin? Was it in 1931 with the "Manchurian incident," or was it "the China incident" of 1937, or Pearl Harbor in 1941? There is no consensus on this matter in Japan. Historians cannot even agree what to call the war, for that depends on when one thinks it began. Right-wing nationalists still use the wartime term *Daitoa Senso,* or Great East Asian War, which began with the attack on the United States. The name implies that Japan fought a war of Asian liberation from Western empires. What happened in China before 1941 is treated as a minor matter, that is, as mere "incidents." Others talk only about the Pacific War, *Taiheiyo Senso,* as though there had been no war apart from the one against the United States. Leftists, critical of their country's wartime past, see the Japanese war as a colonial conquest beginning with the annexation of Manchuria in 1931 and speak of the Fifteen-Year War.

Then there is Hayashi Fusao, who began his intellectual life in the Taisho era as a communist but, like many, ended up as a right-wing nationalist. His revisionist book, *In Affirmation of the Great East Asian War,* written long after the Japanese defeat, offered the thesis that Japan had fought a one-hundred-year war, beginning with the first, unsuccessful American mission, led by James Biddle in 1846. Ever since that day, when Captain Biddle attempted to open relations with Japan and was roughed up by a Japanese guard, Japan had been at war with the West.

Hayashi was echoing propaganda of the 1930s, which always painted Japan as the victim of Western powers, whose wicked bullying forced Japan to stand up for the Asian people. One of the chief architects of Japan's war on

China told his interrogators after 1945 that Commodore Perry and his black ships were really to blame for the whole thing, because Perry had dragged Japan from peaceful isolation into the merciless international system of big-power rivalry. It is a thesis one still comes across in the more reactionary Japanese journals. Since these journals get more attention now than more liberal publications, it would be wise to take note of such views. But whatever one wishes to call the war, there is no doubt that 1931 marked a new beginning of Japanese military aggression on the Asian continent.

The Manchurian incident occurred on September 18, 1931. It could easily have happened earlier. Although a Chinese warlord governed Manchuria as a semi-independent fiefdom, the Japanese were already in a strong position. The Japanese Kwantung army controlled the area along the South Manchurian Railway, which included most of the main cities, such as Harbin and Mukden. The port cities of Dalian and Port Arthur were already under direct Japanese administration. But the army was getting restless and wanted more. The worldwide economic slump was hitting Japan hard, and a violently anticapitalist mood was taking hold of some of the younger officers and men. In Tokyo, right-wing zealots and junior officers were agitating against businessmen and civilian politicians and plotting coups d'états. In China, Chiang Kai-shek's army was moving north in an attempt to unify the nation under a nationalist government. The Chinese saw Manchuria as part of China; the Japanese, despite earlier treaties to that effect, did not. They preferred to see it as a kind of lawless no-man's-land, to which Japan would bring order. Since Manchuria had been part of the last Chinese empire, which lasted for almost three centuries, the Chinese had a legitimate claim. The fact that large parts of China were lawless did not give Japan the right to take them over.

Manchuria in the 1930s was full of bellicose Japanese officers, right-wing dreamers, and revolutionary desperadoes. Lieutenant Colonel Ishiwara Kanji was all of these things. A brilliant baby-faced maverick, he had studied for three years in Germany, where he picked up modish ideas on global racial war. The endgame, in his view, was a titanic struggle between the white and yellow races, with Japan and America as the main adversaries. Like Kita Ikki, the intellectual mentor of military extremists, he was a disciple of Nichiren Buddhism and dreamed of the whole world united under one Japanese imperial roof. But first he plotted a Japanese army takeover of Manchuria, which in due course would be transformed into "paradise."

An earlier plot had failed in 1928, when Kwantung army men blew up the local warlord Chang Tso-lin's train. Blaming it on Chinese soldiers, they had hoped to create an excuse for the Japanese army to take control. It didn't quite come off. Emperor Hirohito, appalled by such disorderly conduct, forced his prime minister to resign, and the affair was effectively hushed up. So this time, in 1931, things would have to be organized better. On the night of September 18, a bomb was set off by Japanese soldiers next to the railway line near Mukden. No real harm was done to South Manchurian Railway property, the trains still ran on time, but it provided the cue for an attack on Chinese troops in Mukden, who were blamed for the "sabotage." In an attempt to calm things down, Chang Hsüeh-liang, who succeeded his father as warlord, told his men not to resist. The Japanese then announced that all Chinese soldiers were bandits, and all bandits Chinese soldiers, and since it was the duty of the Kwantung army to ensure the safety and security of Manchuria, they attacked them anyway. Within six months, much of Manchuria was in Japanese hands. The Chinese complained to the League of Nations. And the Japanese duly cranked out propaganda at home about Japan being victimized by the rest of the world.

The prime minister at the time of the Manchurian incident, Wakatsuji Reijiro, was still a party politician who favored a conciliatory policy toward China. He was in a state of panic. The Kwantung army was pushing Japan toward war, and there was nothing he could do about it, since military affairs were beyond his brief. The army and navy ministers in his cabinet were answerable to the emperor as supreme commander of the armed forces, but not to a mere civilian prime minister. The foreign minister, Shidehara Kijuro, was also an internationalist who tried to maintain good relations with China and the West. He was now in the invidious position of having to defend a fait accompli in Manchuria, caused by military officers over whom the civilian government had no control. The emperor was advised by nervous courtiers and chiefs of staff not to antagonize his armed forces, lest they rebel and create disturbances at home. In a complete abdication of responsibility, the opposition party, the Seiyukai, criticized the government for not being belligerent enough. Meanwhile, Japanese troops began to move into Manchuria from Korea. The prime minister resigned.

His successor, Inukai Tsuyoshi, was no more successful in disciplining the military in China. He tried in vain to withhold official recognition of Manchuria as an "independent" state. Provoked by anti-Japanese sentiments, Japanese marines attacked Chinese troops in Shanghai. When Chinese resistance turned out to be rather more robust than expected, the army was called in to help the marines. The Japanese press stoked up public opinion by publishing glowing reports of Japanese heroism in Shang-hai. Soldiers who died in suicidal actions were glorified as "human bullets."

Inukai, like his predecessor, was a pathetic bystander in these events. He appealed to the emperor to intervene, but nothing happened. After one more attempt to stop Japanese reinforcements from escalating the violence in Shanghai, Inukai was gunned down by navy fanatics in his own house. Henceforth, Japan would be governed by "na-tional unity" cabinets. Of the fourteen prime ministers who governed Japan between 1932 and 1945, only four were civilians. This had been the aim all along, not just of plotters like Ishiwara Kanji, but of some of the high-est military officials in Tokyo, who had connived in his schemes. The army and navy ministers were made barons after the "incidents" in Manchuria and Shanghai.

In a way, the 1932 assassination of Inukai, which ended the system of party cabinets, was comparable to the Nazi takeover of Germany in 1933, except that Japan had no Nazi Party and no führer. The emperor was a figure of ab-solute authority, but he was neither a Fascist Party leader nor a military dictator. We still cannot be sure to what ex-tent he was a puppet or an active player in wartime politics, but as long as he was there to provide divine guidance, no one else could become a dictator, either. Many of Japan's problems were the result of weakness and divisions at the pinnacle of the system rather than strength. Far from being a united nation, Japan was ruled by factions, in the court, the military, the bureaucracy, and the Diet, which fought one another with almost as much zeal as they displayed toward external enemies.

Unlike 1933 in Germany, 1932 in Japan was not a complete break in continuity, since the constitution was never abolished. The emperor system put in place after the Meiji Restoration remained intact. The same men who governed Japan before 1932 continued to do so. The political parties continued to exist until 1940, but mostly as cheerleaders or occasionally as spoilers. Since party politicians still took up government posts, and the Diet continued to function, they could break a cabinet by refusing to cooperate. To the degree that their cheers were still needed, they retained a vestige of influence. What had been radically altered was the balance of powers. Until 1932, authority was shared by the court, the bureaucracy, the armed forces, and the Diet. Parliament was always the weakest link but had gained in strength through party-based cabinets in the 1920s. Now that this had come to an end, Japanese politics would be driven by congeries of courtiers, army and navy chiefs, and bureaucrats, whose decisions were often forced on them by fanatical subordinates.

———

One thing that made the strangulation of parliamentary government relatively easy was the power of propaganda. Military aggression in China was, in that early stage, extremely popular in Japan. As with the rise of fascism and national socialism in Europe, Japan's imperial madness was fueled by mass entertainment and the popular press. This was the age of mass politics in Japan no less than in Europe. The economic slump in the 1930s had been devastating for the growing middle class and thus for bourgeois politics. Everything was done to discredit the relative liberalism of the Taisho era. Early Showa was made to resemble the most belligerent years of late Meiji. Emperor Hirohito was compared to his grandfather, the Meiji emperor. His former teacher, General Nogi, and other Meiji heroes were held up as models to follow. *Remember General Nogi* was a huge success on the stage. The brave bugler of the Russo-Japanese War who kept blowing as he staggered forward with a bullet in his lung was celebrated once more in comic books, boys' magazines, and songs. The popular music of the Jazz Age was replaced by marching songs, with such late-Meiji-type titles as "The Imperial Army Marches Off," or "Military Spy Song," or "Ah, Our Manchuria."

All the romantic yearnings, nationalism, and anxieties of an age of great economic depression were poured into the Manchurian project. People were told that Manchuria was the "lifeline" of Japan. Without Manchuria, so the experts said, the Japanese economy, already weakened by the slump, would collapse. Manchuria would offer lebensraum to the Japanese people, and its coal and iron mines would provide vital resources. Heavy industries would be set up and new banks opened. There would be construction of roads, airports, bridges, factories. Cities, more modern, more efficient, more dazzling than anything seen even in Japan, would be built from scratch. Manchuria, with Korea, Taiwan, and other Japanese possessions, would be bound together in a giant yen bloc, not to exploit the people, as happened in the capitalist West, but to bring prosperity to all the emperor's subjects. The economy would be put firmly under government control. Bureaucrats, business leaders, and generals would work harmoniously together to make Manchuria the engine of a great empire.

All this was more wishful than real. The Manchurian project was wrapped in fiction in almost every respect. First of all, it didn't make as much economic sense as experts thought it would. Military planners had different economic priorities from businessmen, so there was con-

stant tension between the army and the *zaibatsu*. The factories, roads, power plants, and dazzling cities were indeed
built at huge expense. Japanese bureaucrats honed their
skills in management of industrial development. And some
businesses got very rich. But after an early boom in trade,
the yen bloc turned out to be more of a drain on the Japanese economy than a boost. Manchuria could not absorb
Japanese exports. Products manufactured in Manchuria
were not good enough to replace Western imports. And the
Japanese state ran out of money to support the industrial
development in Manchuria. So the grand corporate vision
of an imperial powerhouse turned out to be something of
an illusion.

But that was the least of the deceptions. Officially Manchuria, now called Manchukuo, was an independent state,
whose emperor, Henry Pu Yi, the hapless last scion of the
Qing dynasty, would be "advised" by discreet, capable, and
benevolent Japanese officials. Part of the fiction was that
Manchukuo was inhabited mostly by Manchus and not
Chinese. There were actually very few Manchus left, and
even they were usually indistinguishable from the Chinese
majority. The Japanese claimed that China itself was not a
"viable state," and therefore the Japanese had every right
to protect their interests by taking a firm hand in the north.
In fact, no matter how much ceremonial respect was ac-
corded by the Japanese to the last emperor of China, Manchukuo was not even a puppet state, but a colony pure and
simple. Manchukuo officials were Chinese, it is true, but
their appointments and policies were in the hands of the
Kwantung army.

The Chinese government continued to object to this
state of affairs, and the League of Nations sent a mission of
international worthies to Manchukuo to investigate the

merits of the Japanese case. There was still some sympathy, especially in Britain, for Japan. Travel writers and other visitors were struck by the efficiency of the Japanese in Manchukuo and contrasted the neatness, orderliness, and cleanliness of Japanese settlements with the chaos and filth in the Chinese towns. Japanese soldiers could be a trifle rough and arrogant, to be sure, but the railway hotels were splendid, and this was one place, apart from Mussolini's Italy, where the trains always ran on time.

Alas for Japan, the League of Nations mission, led by Lord Lytton, concluded that the Japanese claims were spurious. This elicited another round of self-pitying propaganda: The West was ganging up on Japan together with the Chinese. Old grievances, some not unreasonable, were rehearsed in the press: the soft peace terms for Russia in 1905, the refusal of Western powers to allow Japan to build more battleships in 1921, America's discriminatory immigration policies, and so forth. Much was made once more of the Japanese blood shed "for Manchuria" in the war against Russia. In the end, the Japanese quite literally walked out of the League of Nations, and their chief delegate, Matsuoka Yosuke, made an astonishing speech in which he compared Japan to Jesus Christ, crucified by world opinion.

Yet even in the most militarist of times, it is a mistake to see Japan as monolithic. Old political differences and conflicts were not dead. Right-wing terrorists might have been forcing events, but the Left was still alive, especially in the universities, where Marxists retained a strong voice. A socialist party actually survived until 1940. And almost no Japanese dissidents left the country to go to the West. This is partly because most Japanese could not contemplate life outside Japan. They had neither the languages nor the contacts. But it was also because much was done to help them ease their way into the new order at home. The Japanese authorities didn't use Nazi methods to control potential dissidents. There were no concentration camps for Japanese leftists. Conformity could be made to seem so painless that many intellectuals never even felt they had betrayed their ideals.

Manchukuo was one way out. It became a playground for many left-wing idealists, who found work as researchers or consultants for the railway company, thinking they were helping to reform and modernize the Asian masses. One of the great advantages of model colonies was that one could experiment without public resistance. This made Manchukuo, and also Taiwan, very attractive to architects and engineers. But there was scope for "progressive" social scientists, too, who might have genuinely believed in the official propaganda about making Manchukuo a model of racial harmony. The closest thing to a Manchukuo political party was the Kyowakai, or Concordia Society, which mobilized the "five races"—Japanese, Manchus, Koreans, Chinese, and Russians—to live in harmony and obey Japanese orders. Whatever the other four races thought of this arrangement, as a Japanese you could feel you were freer, and certainly more comfortable, in Dalian or Mukden than in Osaka or Tokyo.

Japanese novelists and essayists flocked to Manchukuo to write about its remarkable modernity, the speed of its trains, the fine parks in Dalian, and the cosmopolitan nightlife in Harbin. Some of the best filmmakers worked for the Manchu film studios, where they were given the most advanced facilities to make movies about brave Japanese pioneers helping their Asian brethren. Many of these artists and writers were in fact Marxists, whose sentiments were anticapitalist and thus anti-Western anyway. Pan-Asianism appealed to their sense of idealism. All they had to do was switch from socialism to a brand of national socialism.

For stubborn dissidents in Japan there was another option, which sometimes involved a certain amount of force, but usually peer or family pressure, or the sheer loneliness of a contrarian position, would do the trick. It was called *tenko*, "conversion." At least one communist writer, Kobayashi Takiji, refused to renounce his political beliefs, and he died in prison in 1933, probably as the result of torture. But this kind of brutality, though by no means unique, was uncommon. Almost all leftists who were jailed for political reasons in the early 1930s renounced communism, without being tortured, and "converted"—that is to say, they promised never to promote Marxism again. After that, most were released and, although they might be spied on by police bullies and denounced by neighbors as "Reds," left unmolested.

Perhaps the saddest reflection on the state of Japanese intellectual life in early Showa was the case of Professor Minobe Tatsukichi. Far from being a dangerous leftist, Minobe was a conservative defender of Taisho democracy. As professor of constitutional law at Tokyo Imperial University, he developed his theory of the emperor as an organ of state. He argued that parliament was not constitutionally bound simply to follow imperial orders. The emperor should not be put in the position of having to make political decisions for which, as head of state, he could not be held accountable. Only a strong Diet, whose political authority was constitutionally guaranteed, would ensure that military figures did not run amok in the emperor's name.

Minobe's prescient views were publicly debated in the

1920s, in the press and in the Diet, and pretty much accepted, at least in theory, even by imperial court circles. Extreme nationalists wrote hostile articles and made threats, but could not dislodge him from his position of authority. Minobe was so much part of the Taisho establishment that he was given a seat in the House of Peers after his retirement as a professor.

Things were different, however, in 1935. When he was denounced by right-wing extremists, and attacked in the House of Peers for lèse-majesté and for damaging the *kokutai,* none of his colleagues felt able to defend him. Minobe lost his position, and his books were banned. The attacks on him were partly personal, the settling of old academic scores, but also political. For the real target of the extremists, in the armed forces and right-wing pressure groups, was not Minobe, but the old establishment, the political parties, of course, and even the imperial court itself. By "clarifying the *kokutai,*" the rightists wanted to do away with wishy-washy courtiers, bickering politicians, and timid bureaucrats who were urging caution on the emperor. The divine military state they envisaged had no room for constitutional interpretations.

The armed forces were divided, however, like every Japanese institution. The two warring factions at the time of the Minobe affair were the Imperial Way faction, Kodoha, and the Control faction, Toseiha. The latter, which included Ishiwara Kanji, the Manchurian plotter, and General Tojo Hideki, saw the future in terms of total war with the West. Staging violent rebellions in Japan against capitalists and bureaucrats was not their style. They believed in military discipline and building national strength in cooperation with the bureaucracy and big business. The Imperial Way men wanted a revolution, a Showa Restoration, which would rid the nation of corrupt capitalists and other enemies of the *kokutai* and create a military dictatorship under a new constitution. The guardians of Japan's precarious imperial system had always feared revolts from the Left. The real threat, however, came from the Right.

In 1935, in the midst of the Minobe affair, military squabbling for government positions turned violent. A top military bureaucrat in the Control faction was about to remove some troublesome Imperial Way officers from their posts. For this he was slashed to death in his office by a young officer wielding a samurai sword. As usual in Japan, the young officer's sincerity was widely admired and much praised in the popular press. To cool things down, some of his most enthusiastic supporters were sent off to Manchukuo, and the Control faction reasserted its authority. Apart from the weather, however, nothing became remotely cooler.

February 26, 1936, saw the heaviest snowfall in thirty years. It was then, in the early morning, that junior Imperial Way officers decided to strike. They were a mixed bunch, including the son of a famous Tokyo comedian. Many of them were from the rural northeast, where the slump had caused the cruelest hardships. Poverty was forcing farming families to sell their young women to pimps who roamed the countryside to supply city brothels. The army, brutal as it was, offered farm boys their only refuge. The brighter ones, fired up by the likes of Kita Ikki, drifted into a kind of imperialist fundamentalism, obsessed with purity and religious worship of the nation.

Over a thousand men tried to take over central Tokyo. The finance minister was assassinated in his bedroom, as were the lord privy seal and the inspector general of military education, a Control faction man. Prime Minister Okada escaped with his life only because the rebels killed his brother-in-law instead by mistake. Tokyo citizens were handed pamphlets filled with emotional rhetoric about the sincere feelings of the rebels.

Some of them may have been impressed, but not Emperor Hirohito. He quite rightly saw the attempted coup as a direct attack on the establishment around him. Allowing young Turks a free hand in Manchuria was one thing, but this kind of insubordination at home had to be stopped. The navy was called in to restore order. The rebels were unable, but only just, to storm the palace to make their sincere feelings known to the emperor directly and take out his "evil advisers." On February 29, the whole thing was over, the rebels surrendered, discipline was imposed, and the Control faction was now firmly in control of the government.

Japan had been saved from violent revolution, but the Control faction dealt a further blow against what was still left of civilian influence in government. The military demanded that new cabinet appointments be approved by the army and navy ministers. Since they had to be serving officers, the armed forces could now make or break any government. Hirota Koki, a relatively moderate diplomat, became the new prime minister. But he had to do the army's bidding. So he raised the military budget and signed an anticommunist alliance with Nazi Germany. The other main news to divert Japanese from military affairs in that year was the strange affair of Abe Sada, a small-time geisha, who strangled her lover in a fit of sexual passion and was found wandering around Tokyo carrying his genitals in her handbag.

In China, the troops were getting restless again. Hirota could not handle them, nor could two of his short-lived successors. The conservatives around the throne, who were not yet ready to contemplate an all-out war in China, looked to one of their own to ensure some kind of stability. Prince Konoe Fumimaro had grown up with Hirohito and was his regular golf partner. A cultivated, rather haughty aristocrat, Konoe had traveled widely, was well connected in the armed forces, and had right-wing intellectual friends, yet he was not a natural warmonger. He was, however, ferociously anticommunist and infected by the more extreme racial prejudices of his time. Like Ishiwara Kanji, the Manchurian plotter, he saw the world in terms of racial conflict between East and West. Any form of liberalism was a horror to him. What he had in mind was a united, totalitarian Japanese state, in which domestic conflicts were abolished. One of the permanent features of east Asian politics is the combination of murderous factionalism and highfalutin rhetoric of absolute unity. It is the vicious circle of all authoritarianism: One always goes with the other.

Prince Konoe, despite his military connections, was no more able to restrain the troops in China than his predecessors. The war with China was never actually declared. It began with the "China incident" on July 7, 1937, when a Japanese private relieved himself in the shadows of the Marco Polo Bridge near Peking and then went off for a walk in a so-called demilitarized zone. The soldier was not away for very long, but since he was presumed to be missing, his commander insisted on combing the area. The Chinese proposed a joint search. The Japanese commander took this as an insult. Violence broke out and spread quickly to other parts of northern China.

Konoe appears to have been of two minds. He wanted to teach the Chinese a lesson and "make them reflect," as they say in east Asia, but a full-scale war seems not to have been his intention. He wrote in his diary: "I have made the decision to control the military by abandoning my neutral position and get public opinion behind me." Since the political parties were no longer able to do anything to affect military behavior, Konoe came up with the particularly bad idea of replacing the remaining parties with one quasi-fascist party, the so-called Imperial Rule Assistance Association (IRAA), as a way of mobilizing public opinion. Carried out in 1940, this was to be the coup de grâce for the last pathetic vestiges of Taisho democracy. It did nothing to control the armed forces.

Before that unhappy event, however, in the summer of 1937, Japanese troops fought a horrendous battle near Shanghai with Chiang Kai-shek's best forces. The city was bombed, and 250,000 Chinese, including many civilians, were killed as the battles raged in the outskirts. A plaque placed near the scene of great massacres mentions that "blood flowed together with the rivers and changed the color of the sea." In November, more Japanese troops landed in the Bay of Hangzhou. A balloon was floated above Shanghai announcing in Chinese that one million Japanese had landed. The bloody march to Chiang Kai-shek's capital of Nanking had begun.

———

The Nanking massacre of December 1937 was undoubtedly one of the worst atrocities of the Japanese war. However, comparing it to the Nazi Holocaust, as some do, is not very helpful in understanding the particular nature of this war crime. It was an orgy of violence more than a planned extermination campaign. Behaving like medieval conquerors, drunken Japanese soldiers roamed the streets with cartloads of loot. Thousands of women of all ages were gang-raped before being killed or mutilated. Entire neighborhoods were put to the torch. Chinese men and boys, tethered like cattle, were machine-gunned into ditches or the Yangtze River, whose banks were clogged with bloated corpses. Civilians were often murdered for the sheer fun of it, used for bayonet practice and other grisly games. And this went on for six weeks. Embarrassed Japanese diplomats sent foreign eyewitness reports to Tokyo, hoping that something would be done to stop it. Nothing was. Right next to the embassy was a girls' school. The diplomats would have been able to hear the screams of students being raped and tortured.

We shall never know exactly how many Chinese died in the massacre. Estimates—often depending on political points of view—range from thousands, to tens of thousands, to more than 300,000. The Tokyo War Crimes Tribunal put the figure at 250,000. But the exact number should not be the main issue. What needs to be explained is the peculiar ferocity of this assault on a defenseless population. If the point was not to exterminate every last Chinese, what then was the reason for this extraordinary frenzy of rape, murder, and pillage? What caused the complete breakdown of discipline in an army that in earlier wars had been known for its orderly behavior? Many answers have been put forward: the pathology of Japanese culture, the Way of the Samurai, and all that; a deliberately planned act of terror, ordered from Tokyo, to force Chiang Kai-shek's government into submission; a massive letting off of steam by brutalized, battle-weary troops.

That the massacre was ordered by the government in Tokyo seems unlikely. The emperor and his advisers were still conscious of international opinion. Japan desperately needed a constant supply of raw materials and industrial exports from Britain and the United States. Washington's policy was to remain neutral, yet public sympathy was on the side of China. This was why Japan had not declared war on China; policing an "incident" seemed less likely to give offense. And America, under its so-called neutrality laws, would have been forced to cease trading with both sides in the event of a declaration of war, cutting off war-related imports neither Japan nor China felt they could easily afford to lose. Upsetting the American public with atrocity stories was, in any case, not in Japan's best interests. And the Japanese generals quickly realized that mass rapes hardened Chinese resistance. To counter that trend, the Japanese War Ministry decided to recruit or, more usually, kidnap Koreans, Chinese, Southeast Asians, and even some Europeans to serve in a vast network of army brothels, or "comfort stations."

Mass murder did follow another Japanese policy, however, which was to take no prisoners. From the moment they landed, Japanese troops were told by their officers to "clear up" captured soldiers as they fought their way up to Nanking. Since there was a lot of guerrilla warfare, the Japanese usually made no distinctions between soldiers and civilians. Brutalized already by ill treatment from their own superior officers, Japanese soldiers were coarsened further by fighting savage battles in a foreign country. All Chinese were enemies in their eyes, including women and children. Rather than feed them, it was simpler just to kill them.

The siege of Nanking had been a particularly brutal affair. Many Japanese lives were lost before Chiang Kai-shek decided to abandon his capital, in a helter-skelter river crossing with much of his army and thousands of mostly privileged citizens in tow. The roughly half a million people left in Nanking included many refugees from the countryside and soldiers in civilian clothes. When Japanese troops, literally drunk with victory, were told to mop up, they had little idea how to distinguish citizens from ex-soldiers. Having callused hands was usually sufficient justification for execution.

Yet this alone does not explain the bestiality of what happened in Nanking. What the Japanese did to the Chinese is more akin to what Hindus and Muslims did to each other in 1947, or what Serbs did to Bosnian Muslims in the 1990s, or indeed what Nazis did to Jews. It was not enough to kill; the victims had to be humiliated and dehumanized first. This makes the killing easier, for it strips the victims of their humanity. But it is also the result of vicious indoctrination. For years, Japanese had been told the Chinese were inferior and the Japanese a divine race. Contempt for the Chinese goes back to those Meiji prints of the Sino-Japanese War, in which the Japanese are tall, white, and vigorous and the Chinese are cowering yellow cretins. Government propaganda, parroted by the jingoistic Japanese press, told soldiers they were fighting a holy war. Anything they did in the name of the emperor, no matter how savage, was sanctioned by the holiness of their cause. An American chaplain in Tokyo's Sugamo prison, where Japanese war criminals were held after the war, concluded from his many interviews that they "had the belief that any enemy of the emperor could not be right, so the more brutally they treated their prisoners, the more loyal to the emperor they were being."

Nanking was probably the worst single atrocity, but there would be many more, in China, Manchukuo, the Philippines, Singapore, Malaya, Thailand, Indonesia, and Burma. It was as though the militarist monster, forged in late Meiji from a mixture of late Edo nativism and borrowed German racial theories, had finally burst into horrible life. This was the result of a sequence of human decisions and wrong paths taken that long preceded the reign of Emperor Hirohito. It was also a sign of a hopelessly flawed chain of command, where thugs in the field overruled their superior officers, junior officers in Tokyo intimidated generals, and chiefs of staff bullied civilian bureaucrats and the imperial court.

There was little sign in Tokyo that something ghastly had happened. The emperor commended his generals for a job well done. The one man to show any remorse for Nanking was General Matsui Iwane, who was in charge of the Central China Area Army when the nationalist capital was taken. After Nanking he resigned his position, shaved his head, and went into a Buddhist retreat. During his trial after the war, he called the massacre "a national disgrace," and yet he was hanged while many of his junior officers who gave the actual orders on the scene went unpunished.

———

Even as the emperor's troops got bogged down in China, skirmishes on the borders of Manchukuo and the Soviet Union were threatening to get out of control. Officers of the Kwantung army, such as Colonel Tsuji Masanobu, a maniacal soldier responsible for all manner of outrages before the war was over, were itching to attack the Soviet army. Tsuji was a proponent of the Strike North faction, as were most members of the Imperial Way. They wanted to contain the Soviet Union by taking control of eastern Siberia. General Araki Sadao, who was, rather absurdly, Prince Konoe's education minister, once said that if the Soviets did not cease to annoy Japan, he would "have to purge Siberia as one cleans a room of flies."

The Strike North faction was largely army based and at-

tracted many junior officers. Those who wished to avoid a
war with the Soviet Union and head south instead, where
control of the rich natural resources of Southeast Asia
would allow the navy to build up strength for an eventual
war in the Pacific, were mostly admirals, generals, and
high-ranking officers of the Control faction. The emperor
had no desire to go to war with the Soviets and was on the
whole more sympathetic to the navy. There was, however,
no consensus at all about what to do next: cut a deal with
Chiang Kai-shek and retreat from China proper; patch
things up with the West; prepare for an all-out war with
the West; prop up a Chinese puppet regime in Nanking;
get even closer to Nazi Germany; strengthen the army,
strengthen the navy; strike north, strike south. But as so
often happened, Tokyo's dog was wagged by its military
tail, once more in Manchuria.

Fighting broke out in the summer of 1938 on the wet
and misty borderlands of Korea, Manchukuo, and the Soviet Union. Soviet troops were building a fortification on
the Manchukuo side of the Tumen River, and the Japanese
decided to test them. The Soviets had bombers and tanks.
The Japanese had none, but they set great store on their
superior "spirit." After battling for a fortnight, there were
many dead on both sides, more on the Japanese than the
Russian, but nothing much was gained or lost. The emperor told his general staff to stop the war. Colonel Tsuji
ordered his men to go on regardless. Spirit would see them
through. Less than a year later, at Nomonhan, on the bor-
der with Outer Mongolia, the Japanese, armed with Molo-
tov cocktails, sabers, field guns, and some light tanks,
attacked General Zhukov's Soviet tank brigades. The fighting on ghastly, mosquito-infested terrain went on for
months and ended in a slaughter. The flatlands were filled

with Japanese corpses, feasted on by black desert vultures. More than twenty thousand Japanese died of hunger, thirst, and disease, as well as from Russian bombardments. Colonel Tsuji was duly promoted. But the plan to strike north was abandoned. From then on all the action would be to the south.

5

WAR AGAINST THE WEST

It was a moment of great joy for the emperor and many of his subjects when Japanese torpedo and dive bombers wrecked much of the U.S. fleet at Pearl Harbor on December 7, 1941. Emperor Hirohito was dressed for the occasion in his navy uniform, and courtiers recorded that His Majesty was in "a splendid mood." Hayashi Fusao, author of *In Affirmation of the Great East Asian War,* was traveling in Manchukuo when he heard the news. It was, he wrote, "as if a heavy load had been lifted from my shoulders." Takamura Kotaro, the poet, sculptor, and Parisian-style bohemian, wept tears of joy. The literary critic Ito Sei "felt as if in one stroke I had become a new man. . . ." After Pearl Harbor came Singapore, the Dutch East Indies, the Philippines . . . The holy war (*seisen*) of Asian liberation could not have got off to a better start.

One Japanese eyewitness, Okuna Takao, a distinguished literary critic, summed it up as follows:

"The attitudes of ordinary people, who had felt ambivalent about the war against China, and even of intellectuals who denounced it as an invasion, were transformed as soon as the war against Britain and the U.S. began. . . . Everyone worried about what would happen to Japan. . . . At the same time, there was a sense of euphoria that we'd done it at last; we'd landed a punch on those arrogant great powers Britain and America, on those white fellows. As the news of one victory after another came in, the worries faded, and fear turned to pride and joy. . . . All the feelings of inferiority of a colored people from a backward country, towards white people from the developed world, disappeared in that one blow. . . . Never in our history had we Japanese felt such pride in ourselves as a race as we did then."

This is probably as truthful a description as one is ever likely to get. All those years of being told one was the victim of the arrogant West, all the snubs and slights, real or not, the humiliations of trying to catch up with the material superiority, not to mention the "Civilization and Enlightenment," of the Occident by acting as the best pupils in the class of Westernization—the shame of all that had been wiped out in one blow by those dive bombers swooping down on Pearl Harbor. Perhaps now the world would take the Japanese as seriously as they took themselves.

After the first victories in 1937, more and more Japanese had been troubled by the "holy war" in China. Japanese war movies of the time were surprisingly honest in showing hardships suffered by the common soldiers—though not, with rare exceptions, of their victims. Wartime propaganda rarely focused on the wickedness of Japan's enemies. Films celebrated the spirit of self-sacrifice, of everyone doing his bit for the nation, the poor soldiers stuck in the Chinese mud as much as the people back home. There was no joy in the seemingly endless battles and skirmishes in China, which never produced the desired result of Chinese submission. The government didn't appear to know what to do, and besides, all the propaganda about a new Asian order, based on fraternal love and cultural kinship, sounded hollow as long as Japanese were fighting fellow Asians, no matter how inferior they were deemed to be to the sons of the divine empire.

Until the war with the West, Tokyo was still a pretty Westernized place. People played baseball, even though American baseball terminology was being laboriously replaced with Japanese phrases. Hollywood movies were shown. People listened to Western music, classical and modern, and read Western books. German and Italian music and books were never proscribed. What was purged from Japanese life between 1941 and 1945 was the West associated with the "Anglo-Saxons"—that is to say, everything Japanese liberals since the Meiji Restoration had admired and tried to emulate. The Japanese war was, among many other things, a war against liberalism.

The political parties, whose voices had been largely stifled already, were dissolved in 1940 and replaced by the Imperial Rule Assistance Association, designed to make "one hundred million hearts beat as one," from the chiefs of staff down to the lowliest (but invariably bossy) block leaders of local neighborhood associations. There were still Diet elections, but the candidates were almost all reliable hard-line nationalists put forward by the IRAA. An extreme form of emperor worship was imposed in every institution, beginning with the primary schools. At the mere mention of the emperor, people were required to jump to attention. The Japanese spirit was turned into a quasi-religious cult. People were told that self-denial, endurance, and sacrifice were uniquely Japanese virtues, hence those many war movies focusing on hardship. Spiritual strength and sheer force of will would overcome all material obstacles.

Racial purity was as much a part of wartime propaganda in Japan as it was in Germany, though not with quite the same genocidal consequences. Since the official target of Japanese propaganda was liberalism, in the sense of individualism, pluralism, materialism, capitalism, and democracy, Japan and Germany were fighting the same idea of the West. But while the Nazis saw Jews as the embodiment of all these evils, the Japanese were told to smash the "Anglo-American beasts" represented by Churchill and Roosevelt, depicted in cartoons as depraved top-hatted plutocrats. The English language itself was thought to be a form of pollution. One wartime cartoon shows a Japanese student dumping his English phrases ("You are a dog") into a rubbish bin, while his mother, in the manner of a Shinto priest, sprinkles purifying salt around.

After almost a hundred years of Westernization, the Japanese were now to be Asians with a vengeance. Not only would the Imperial Armed Forces fight a holy war to kick the white man out of Asia, but all vestiges of Western, liberal thinking would be purged from Asian minds. This new Asianism was as overwrought and false as the Westernized manners of waltzing and whist-playing grandees in the early Meiji years. Intellectuals and military propagandists used such phrases as "overcoming modernity" or "overcoming the West," as though the two meant the same thing, and the whole modern project in Japan had to be turned upside down. One can see why the self-aggrandizing idea of Asian pride, embodied by Japan as the philosophical and political mentor of all Asian peoples, had a strong emotional appeal. But the new Japanese order, though in part an extreme version of eighteenth- and nineteenth-century nativism, owed as much to Western ideas as did the Marxism of Taisho-period intellectuals. Much of it was borrowed from European fascism and grafted onto more east Asian habits of thought.

However, Nazi Germany and Japan were not the same. National socialism was a revolutionary idea, carried out by a populist party. The Japanese elite, in the military, imperial court, business, and bureaucracy, used a form of fascism to impose order on an enterprise that was forever threatening to get out of hand. The Control faction in the armed forces, represented by General Tojo and backed by the emperor, tried to stay ahead of the more radical Imperial Way faction to avoid a revolution. Hitler and his satraps already had grandiose designs on the world before they came to power. The Japanese elite, beyond sharing a dislike for liberalism in all its forms, seemed to be cobbling together their political dogmas to justify an endless string of faits accomplis. And at least some of them knew even before the attack on Pearl Harbor that Japan had embarked on a mission of national suicide.

—

Why, then, did they do it? What possessed Admiral Yamamoto Isoroku, who had warned Prime Minister Konoe that Japan could successfully challenge the United States for one year at the most, to go along with the attack on Pearl Harbor? Again, the most likely explanation is not a führer's diktat, as in Germany's attack on the Soviet Union, but weakness, even paralysis, at the highest levels of Japanese government. If few deeply desired a war with the West, nobody, except possibly the emperor himself, was able or willing to stop it.

Preliminaries to the final showdown began in January 1940, when the United States, "in the interests of national defense," stopped selling aviation fuel and scrap metal to Japan. The Japanese knew that this would make it impossible for them to maintain their military presence in China for long. The Americans were aware of this, too, hence their new policy. Further restrictions on all grades of iron and steel scrap followed. Japan had a clear choice now: to withdraw from China or move into Southeast Asia for its raw materials. Since military control of China was deemed essential to Japan's national survival, the first option was out of the question. Germany invaded France. Japan then burned more bridges with the United States by joining the Axis powers. In July 1941, Japanese troops occupied southern Indochina. The Americans, as well as the British and the Dutch, now decided to block the export of oil. Japanese newspapers, in their usual tone of victimhood, reported that Japan's lifeline was being strangled by the ABCD powers: American, British, Chinese, and Dutch.

Japan could still withdraw from China, but General Tojo, the minister of war, said there could be "no compromise on the stationing of troops in China. . . ." Since the armed forces could not carry on without oil, this meant going for the oil-rich Dutch East Indies. There was, of course, one other option, suggested by the naval chief of staff, Admiral Nagano Osami, five days before the U.S. oil embargo. Since time was running out, and the navy was consuming four hundred tons of oil a day, Japan should attack the United States immediately, for that would offer the best "chance of achieving victory." If the Japanese occupied the Philippines, the navy would surely be able to control the Pacific.

Admiral Nagano was still a little ahead of his colleagues, however. Neither the emperor, nor Tojo, nor Konoe wanted to take on the United States, or at any rate not just yet. It was decided to string out diplomatic negotiations while preparing for a possible war. Various proposals were put to Washington. Japan would withdraw from Indochina once the "China incident" had been settled to Japan's satisfaction and economic sanctions were lifted. Or Japan would consider making peace with China, as long as Japanese troops could stay in China to guarantee regional security. Or Japan promised not to grab other parts of Southeast Asia, if oil supplies could be resumed. None of these proposals found a positive response. What to do now? The Japanese leaders decided to wait until October. If the

Americans hadn't seen it Japan's way by then, war would be inevitable.

October came. Konoe invited the army and navy ministers, the foreign minister, and the president of the planning board, Suzuki Teiichi, to his private residence. General Suzuki described this fateful meeting at the Tokyo trials five years later: "It became quite clear as the result of this conference where the thorny question lay. The Navy really thought that the war with America was impossible but did not desire openly to say so. The Army did not necessarily desire war, but vigorously objected to the withdrawal of troops from China. The Foreign Minister was firmly of the opinion that without consenting to the withdrawal of the armed forces from China, the negotiation with America offered no prospect of success. The only way for the Prime Minister to avoid war was, therefore, either to make the Navy formally declare its real intentions, or to make the Army understand the unexpressed intentions of the Navy and agree to the withdrawal of the armed forces. I saw that the Prime Minister was in a predicament because personally he felt himself unequal to the task of persuading the Navy or the Army." *

No one, in other words, felt able to take responsibility for a coherent policy. The prime minister had no sway over the armed forces. And the army and navy ministers were content to let things drift. The ultimate price was about to be paid for having destroyed the authority of civilian government. The political scientist Maruyama Masao has explained the Japanese catastrophe as the logical outcome of systemic irresponsibility. The emperor, in his view, was

* From Masao Maruyama's *Thought and Behaviour in Modern Japanese Politics*, edited by Ivan Morris (Oxford: Oxford University Press, 1969).

like a portable shrine, carried on the shoulders of men who had no idea where they were going but simply reacted to the latest twists of fortune, as though politics were like the weather: a rainstorm here, a spell of bright weather there, and then, suddenly, a terrible earthquake. The word *kamikaze,* "divine wind," refers to just such a natural phenomenon in the thirteenth century, when a typhoon blew the fleet of Mongol invaders against the rocks. Whenever they were faced with a desperate situation—Commodore Perry's arrival in 1853 or the U.S. victories in 1944—Japanese leaders called for a divine wind to save the nation. Just as no one could be held responsible for the earthquakes that destroyed Japanese cities with ghastly regularity, nobody could feel responsible for making war on the West, except possibly the emperor, but then he was a mere shrine.

It is impossible to say how accurate General Suzuki's account was of the meeting in Konoe's villa. After all, some military figures had been spoiling for a fight. And Professor Maruyama's analysis may be a little too schematic. But that there was a systemic problem is clear. The lack of political accountability made it very easy to blame the fate of hundreds of millions on factors beyond human, or at least Japanese, control, on abstractions like "the inevitable forces of history," or on the ABCD strangulation, or simply on one single American act, such as the famous note from the secretary of state, Cordell Hull, handed to the Japanese ambassador in Washington on November 26, 1941. By that time, Konoe had been replaced as prime minister by General Tojo, who was also war and interior minister.

The Hull note was a "draft mutual declaration of policy." The United States demanded a Japanese withdrawal from Indochina and China, without specifying when or from which parts of China. There was no mention of Manchukuo or Korea. General Tojo presented this note to his government as an ultimatum, which it was not. It was in fact the Japanese who had already given Washington an ultimatum. If the United States had not lifted economic sanctions by November 15, in exchange for vague promises of Japanese troop withdrawals "after a suitable interval" once "peace was established" in China, Japan would go to war. The Hull note was just an excuse. The plan for an attack on Pearl Harbor had already been made. Navy bombers had been practicing the raid over and over in Kagoshima Bay. The man with the greatest doubts, Admiral Yamamoto, had worked it out down to the tiniest details. He went along with the hope that a devastating shock would mollify American demands at the negotiation table. A show of Japanese spirit would surely be enough to make the decadent, materialist Americans see sense. If not, well, as General Tojo observed: "Sometimes people have to shut their eyes and take the plunge."

———

Although the Japanese never had a policy of racial extermination, their holy war in Asia did involve extraordinary cruelty. Prisoners of war were tortured and often worked to death. Southeast Asian slave workers were treated even worse than the Western POWs. Hundreds of thousands died of thirst, starvation, and maltreatment along railway lines and on other hard-labor projects. Gruesome medical experiments were carried out on Chinese and some Europeans by special units in China and Manchukuo. Women and girls from Korea, China, and Southeast Asia were forced to work in military brothels; many died, and survivors were often maimed or traumatized for life. There were massacres of civilians in China, Singapore, Malaya, the Philippines, Burma, and elsewhere. The military police, or Kempeitai, was one of the most brutal outfits of the twentieth century.

The holy war took its toll on the Japanese, too. Food became scarcer in the homelands. Rice was already rationed a year before the attack on Pearl Harbor. Deaths from tuberculosis, already high in Japan, went up from about 140,000 a year in the late 1930s to more than 170,000 in 1943. Block leaders and other busybodies informed the thought police or the Kempeitai of any signs of "defeatist" or "anti-*kokutai*" behavior. People with family connections in the United States, or who had once lived there themselves, were arbitrarily arrested as "spies." Just the merest suspicion of "foreign behavior" could be enough for a nasty session with the secret police. Women were made to wear rustic "native" dress. Children were taught how to die like soldiers. There was growing resentment in Japan about the oppressiveness and austerity of the militarized life, but people were told to conquer any lingering nostalgia for prewar liberties and comforts with the much vaunted Japanese spirit.

The brutality of Japanese military government, at home and abroad, was made all the more sinister by the propaganda of peace and love. The *Kokutai no Hongi,* or *Fundamentals of the National Polity,* promised that Japan would gather the whole world under one imperial roof (*hakko ichi-u*). When Japan joined the Axis powers in 1940, an imperial edict announced: "To enhance justice on earth and make of the world one household is the great injunction, bequeathed by Our Imperial Ancestors, which We lay to heart day and night." Prime Minister Konoe said in that same year that the "basic aim of Japan's national policy lies in the firm establishment of world peace in accordance with the lofty spirit of *hakko ichi-u....*" In 1942, General

Tojo said that the new Asian order would be established "on the basis of moral righteousness," with "Japan at its core."

In 1943, representatives from all parts of the Great East Asian Co-Prosperity Sphere gathered for a conference in Tokyo. Wang Ching-wei was there, representing the collaborationist Chinese government in Nanking, along with José Laurel from the Philippines, Ba Maw from Burma, and the Bengali nationalist Subhas Chandra Bose. Respect for national independence and national traditions was solemnly promised. The Asian delegates posed for a group photograph, with General Tojo in the middle, smiling like a benign patriarch. An official statement was issued: "This Great East Asia Proclamation shows clearly the shared ideals of all Asian peoples. The Great East Asian project is based entirely on justice, and is opposed to the exploitative, aggressive, exclusionary egotism of Britain and America. It will stand as a great lesson that will be revealed to all the peoples of the world."

The Japanese knew they could not build an east Asian empire with military force alone, so they combined promises of national liberation from Western colonial oppression with a peculiar universal version of Japanese essentialism. The uniqueness of the Japanese spirit would, as it were, be exported to enlighten others. It was as if Japanese propagandists sought to reverse the process of cultural transmission. After centuries of having absorbed the cultures of China and the West, Japan would now compel others to imbibe the culture of Japan. Meiji-era idealists talked about Japan as a teacher of Western modernization. Now those lessons would be strictly Japanese. Shinto shrines were built all over the empire. Koreans and Taiwanese were forced to adopt Japanese names. A generation of Indonesian, Burmese, and Filipino schoolchildren were taught from textbooks about the samurai spirit. It never worked, of course. Uniqueness cannot be exported. Most Asians didn't want to be Japanese anyway. And even those who had looked to the Japanese as liberators and teachers changed their minds when the Japanese army imposed its imperial blessings with brute force.

———

Meanwhile, the Americans got closer and closer to the Japanese homeland. Factional and institutional rivalries inside Japan's armed services, as well as the traditional fuzziness in its chain of command, made a mess of the country's war effort. But even if Japan had been led by military geniuses, which it wasn't, this was a war it could never have won. America simply produced more planes, ships, and other necessary matériel, faster and more efficiently than Japan. Keeping their troops in China was already hard enough for the Japanese. It was impossible for them to defend their positions in Southeast Asia and the Pacific. Japan ran out of everything: oil, fighter planes, food. All it had was people, and after the bombing of the homeland began, that, too, was a rapidly diminishing asset.

Guadalcanal fell in 1942, Tarawa in 1943; the next year it was Kwajalein, then Leyte, Luzon, Guam, Saipan, and finally Iwo Jima, from where B-29 bombers were within easy reach of Japanese cities, which they proceeded to demolish one by one. A Japanese officer wrote a poem about what it was like in Guadalcanal:

> Covered in mud from our falls
> Blood oozes from our wounds
> No cloth to bind our cuts
> Flies swarm to the scabs

No strength to brush them away
Fall down and cannot move
How many times have I thought of suicide.

Suicide was the sacrifice demanded of all Japanese soldiers who were captured by the enemy. But it was demanded of civilians, too. By 1944, Japanese leaders knew that the war could not be won by conventional means, but diehards maintained that even if all Japanese had to die, the *kokutai* would survive forever. There could be no surrender. Thus an ancient privilege of the samurai caste became a national duty. When the Americans landed on Saipan, women and children were made to jump off the cliffs. Up to 170,000 civilians died in Okinawa. Thousands were driven into American machine-gun fire as cover for Japanese troops. Others were forced to make room in hiding places for soldiers by killing themselves and their families with razors, knives, or, if necessary, their bare hands. Hundreds of thousands more perished in the man-made firestorms of Tokyo, Osaka, or Fukuoka, and still Japan's Götterdämmerung was being blamed by the ruling elite on the insufficient spirit and loyalty of ordinary citizens.

Schoolchildren were ordered to write letters to Japanese soldiers at the front, telling them to "die gloriously." In 1945, military suicide tactics actually became national policy. The Divine Wind Special Attack Units were the brainchild of Admiral Onishi Takijiro, who committed suicide himself after Japan's defeat. Young men, often from the best universities, were pressured into volunteering for this last show of Japanese spirit. Submarines and fighter planes were constructed especially for the suicide missions. In fact, even though only one in three suicide fighters actually hit an American target, the tactic was damaging to

U.S. ships and cost many lives. But even Admiral Onishi cannot have seriously thought it would win the war. He may have hoped that such tactics would, in the words of one elder statesman, develop a more "advantageous war situation," forcing the enemy to come to terms. The desired effect was certainly deadly, but it was also theatrical: A peculiar idea of Japaneseness, whose seeds were sown in the late Edo period but which became a national pathology in the late 1930s, had turned from outward aggression to pure self-destruction.

There was really just one man who could have put an earlier end to all this misery, and that was the emperor himself. Any decision by his war cabinet had to be unanimous; otherwise the government would fall. And on the all-important matter of ending the war, Hirohito's ministers were far from unanimous. In May 1945, Truman reiterated the Allied position that Japan surrender without conditions, after which the Allies would replace the militarist regime with a democratic government. Much against the wishes of Japan experts in the State Department, including the former ambassador to Tokyo, Joseph Grew, no promise was made to protect the imperial throne. Since the throne was the holiest shrine of the *kokutai,* the emperor was no more keen to accept an unconditional surrender than were his generals.

In June 1945, the imperial palace in Tokyo was hit by a bomb. Perhaps it was this that helped to concentrate the emperor's mind, or perhaps it was worrying reports that his subjects were beginning to get restless. The emperor had been startled by the lack of reverence—indeed, the air of almost hostile indifference—of the bombed-out people when he was whisked through the blackened ruins of central Tokyo. By this time the capital, as well as almost every other major city in Japan, was reduced to heaps of rubble. There was no sign of a civilian rebellion as yet, but the possibility could not be dismissed. Prince Konoe, the former prime minister, warned darkly of a communist revolution that would be an even greater threat to the *kokutai* than an Allied victory.

So the emperor decided to sue for peace without endangering his own divine right to rule. Overtures were made to Stalin, to see whether the Soviets could broker a peace. But Japanese offers were too vague and had come too late. The Soviets were not interested. Even as envoys went back and forth to Moscow, preparations were made for a fight to the end. What was left of the Japanese military industry cranked up production of human torpedoes, suicide planes, human rocket bombs, and special "crash boats" for a final clash to the death with the invaders.

At the Potsdam Conference in July, Truman told Stalin about his "new weapon of unusual destructive force." Stalin already knew this from his spies, so he smiled his crocodile smile and wished the Americans good luck with it. The Potsdam Proclamation, issued by Truman, Churchill, and Chiang Kai-shek, demanded an unconditional surrender. Still, no guarantees were given about the preservation of the throne, but the Allies promised to install a government "in accordance with the freely expressed will of the Japanese people." Some Japanese, such as Foreign Minister Togo Shigenori, realized this was the best Japan could hope for. To have insisted on accepting Allied terms, however, could have landed him and his like-minded colleagues in jail as "defeatists." The military supreme command was still adamant to persevere to the end. Prime Minister Suzuki Kantaro, a retired admiral, did what Japanese leaders had done so often before: He let things drift. The Potsdam Proclamation was ignored, Japanese preparations for a final battle continued, and on August 6 Truman unleashed his special weapon on the city of Hiroshima. In a flash, one hundred thousand, or possibly more, men, women, and children died. Two days later, Soviet troops invaded Manchukuo. Three days after the bombing of Hiroshima, Nagasaki was pulverized, too.

That night, after the news of the Nagasaki bombing had struck home, the emperor convened a meeting inside a stifling underground bunker with his Supreme War Leadership Council. The six members of the council sweated in their dress uniforms, while the emperor, sitting stiffly in front of a gilded screen, listened to their arguments. If consensus could not be reached on how to proceed, the government would fall and many more people would die. What followed was the grotesque culmination of a politics based on mystical dogma. All members agreed on one thing, the preservation of the *kokutai*. There was no agreement, however, on the meaning of that elusive thing. Foreign Minister Togo saw the imperial institution in terms of a secular, constitutional monarchy, an organ of state, as defined by the eminent Taisho-era jurist Minobe Tatsukichi. But his army and navy colleagues regarded the emperor's prerogatives in a divine light. His right to rule could not be compromised. Furthermore, the army minister would not accept an Allied occupation of Japan, let alone a war crimes tribunal.

So it had come down to this. Now that Japan faced total destruction after half a century of wars, it was down to a fundamental question about the definition of the Japanese polity. Millions of American, Chinese, European, Southeast Asian, and Japanese lives hinged on it. Admiral Suzuki, a vague Japanese consensus seeker of the old school, turned to the emperor to decide. The emperor still fretted about the sacred mystique of his office. If the enemy were to land near Ise Bay, they would be able to take over two of the most important Shinto shrines, where the sacred imperial regalia were kept. Under these circumstances, he later remembered thinking, protection of the *kokutai* would be difficult. He made the "sacred judgment" that Allied terms should be accepted.

On August 15, millions of Japanese, many of them sobbing on their knees, heard the emperor's voice for the first time, on the radio. Many could barely understand his formal court language. The contents of his surrender speech were couched in terms similar to those of the Great East Asia propaganda. It was not just to stop further use of "a new and most cruel bomb" that he had decided Japan should surrender, but "to pave the way for a grand peace for all generations to come by enduring the unendurable and suffering what is insufferable."

The emperor left much unsaid. He did not mention the threat of a Soviet invasion or his anxieties about a rebellion among his own people. Like the war itself, its ending was seen by many Japanese as divine providence. But such providence too can be manipulated. Admiral Yonai, a member of the Supreme War Leadership Council, gave a candid account on August 12, 1945: "I think the term is perhaps inappropriate, but the atomic bombs and the Soviet entry into the war are, in a sense, gifts from the gods. This way we don't have to say that we quit the war because of domestic circumstances."

Japan was in ruins. Domestic circumstances would never be the same again. Together with millions of lives buried under the wreckage of war, a particular idea of Japan, both modern and archaic, Western and nativist, destructive of others and of the Japanese themselves, lay buried, too, one hoped forever. Yet there would be times in subsequent years when it still stirred—the last spasms of death, or the lingering signs of a longer-lasting life? Perhaps it is still too early to tell.

6

TOKYO BOOGIE-WOOGIE

General Douglas MacArthur arrived at Atsugi naval airdrome, near Yokohama, on August 30, 1945. Having emerged from his aircraft, the supreme commander for the Allied powers (SCAP) paused at the top of the steps, stuck one hand in his hip pocket, tightened his jaws around his corncob pipe, and surveyed the conquered land through his aviator sunglasses. This trademark pose, casually imperious, had been well rehearsed. It was repeated several times from different angles, so all the press photographers could get a decent shot.

We cannot know exactly what went through SCAP's mind at that moment, but reports of his monologues on the long flight from Australia suggest that he felt like a man with a mission. MacArthur was no expert on Japan; in fact, he knew very little about the place. But guided, in his own account, by George Washington, Abraham Lincoln, and Jesus Christ, he would deliver this benighted Oriental nation from slavery and feudalism and transform its people into pacific democrats. It was to be the most radical overhaul since the Meiji Restoration, another new dawn to the West. But this time America, and not Germany, would be the model, the only model. Officially, the occupation of Japan was to be shared by the other Allied powers, including the Soviet Union. In fact, it was an American show from the start.

SCAP's mission began almost one hundred years after Commodore Perry arrived with his black ships. Then, too, "the universal Yankee nation" had come (in Perry's mind, at any rate) to bring light to Japanese darkness. The guns on the deck of his flagship, *Powhatan*, made sure the Japanese got the message. This earlier mission was not forgotten at the hour of Japan's official surrender. Perry's flag, carefully preserved at the Naval Academy in Annapolis, was flown to Japan for the ceremony on the battleship *Missouri*. After the old flag was hoisted and MacArthur spoke grandiloquently, like the ham actor he was, of freedom, tolerance, and justice, fifteen hundred U.S. Navy fighter planes and four hundred B-29 bombers roared overhead in tight formation.

The Imperial Japanese Army and Navy were disbanded. Leftover stockpiles and matériel were either destroyed or disappeared into the black markets, thus setting up the careers of well-connected Japanese gangsters, political fixers, and right-wing politicians. Destroying Japan's military was only the beginning, however. Political institutions had to be reformed and the *zaibatsu* tackled. The Japanese bureaucracy, on the other hand, was left largely in place to carry out SCAP's reforms for him. Unlike Germany, Japan was to be administered by the Japanese themselves, with SCAP and his staff as puppet masters, frequently moving in the dark. There was a general election in 1946, and occupied Japan continued to be run officially by Japanese governments under the autocratic gaze of SCAP. Thus, an important link between prewar, wartime, and postwar Japan was preserved. The effect was not all to the good.

But SCAP's mission was to be something more profound and grandiose than political reform. Japanese culture itself, the entire cluster of Japanese mentalities grown over thousands of years like noxious weeds, had to be overhauled, cleansed, and remade. SCAP was advised in these matters by some conservative members of his entourage who prided themselves on their knowledge of "the Japanese mind." These were, by and large, conservative men who regarded the Japanese as childlike people, prone to savagery if they were not taken firmly in hand. MacArthur, though not all his advisers, took seriously his duty to impose democracy, but this would involve much more than politics. He saw himself as a reformer of the Japanese soul.

MacArthur's remark in 1951, that in terms of modern civilization the Japanese were like a twelve-year-old boy, was typical of his thinking. The context of this remark, made to a joint committee in the U.S. Senate, is worth repeating. MacArthur was comparing Japan to Germany. The Germans, he said, were a "mature race." The Japanese were still in "a very tuitionary condition." Science, culture, and religion were as highly developed in Germany as in other Western nations. The Nazi poison could be drained from German society without changing German culture, which had after all produced Luther, Beethoven, and Goethe. The Nazi regime had been a perversion of German culture; its leaders had acted brutally in a deliberate attempt to dominate the world. The Germans did not have to be tutored in the ways of another civilization. (MacArthur did not mean this as a compliment; in his view the Germans were all the more despicable because they should have known better.) The Japanese, on the other hand, had behaved like the children they were. They had, in MacArthur's version of events, "stumbled" into militarism because they didn't know any better. This also implied that the Japanese, in their immature state, were still flexible enough to improve under firm and fair guidance.

In the 1850s, Commodore Perry had also done some thinking about the Japanese mind and made the following report to his superiors in the Navy Department: "I was well aware that the more exclusive I should make myself and the more exacting I might be, the more respect these people of forms and ceremonies would be disposed to award me, hence my object, and the sequel will show the correctness of these conclusions." SCAP took exactly the same view, and from the moment he emerged from his plane at Atsugi airdrome to the moment he left in 1951, he hardly saw any Japanese apart from the emperor and other dignitaries in highly formal settings. Aloof and grand to the point of absurdity, SCAP made speeches at them and delivered decrees, but he remained as remote as Japanese rulers traditionally had been from their subjects. The great democratic teacher was as unassailable as the emperor himself.

The parallel was not lost on the Japanese, but they had to be discreet about it. In 1946, a vaudeville performer in Tokyo sang a song that contained the lines "Everybody is talking about democracy. But how can we have a democracy with two emperors?" SCAP's officials were tipped off, and the song was banned. At the Kabuki theater in Tokyo, a particularly fine performance of one of the star actors elicited admiring cries from the audience. "The best in Edo [Tokyo]!" shouted one. "The best in Japan!" yelled another. "General MacArthur!" bellowed a third, after which there was silence, for no one could think of anything more exalted. There was the other emperor, of course, but to shout his name in the theater would have been highly inappropriate, and besides, Japanese knew that SCAP was the ruler now, not Hirohito, who was under the general's protection. For the emperor, too, was a pupil of the Americans, groomed to be the symbol of Japan's transformation. To some, his continued occupation of the imperial throne was a sign of American wisdom; it showed SCAP's shrewd understanding of the Japanese mind. To others, including many Japanese liberals, for whom Japan's wartime defeat meant their own liberation, it was seen as SCAP's most damaging failure.

————

The key word in the early years of the occupation for everything that was wrong with Japanese culture was "feudalism." The Kabuki theater, it was believed, was infested with feudalism. The Nō, austere and aristocratic, and the popular Bunraku puppet theater were, for some reason, judged less harshly. Kabuki plays featuring loyal samurai or scenes of suicide were temporarily banned or heavily censored. So was the *Kojiki,* an eighth-century compilation of myths, some of them extolling the virtues of ancient emperors. Mount Fuji, a sacred spot in Shinto worship, was also marked as a noxious symbol of feudalism. Shots of the famous mountain were cut from Japanese films. Samurai movies were, of course, banned outright.

Teachers who had told a generation of children that the Japanese imperial house was divine and that to die for the emperor was glorious were now instructed to repudiate all that and teach the virtues of *demokurashii* instead. Since it was impossible to print new textbooks immediately, offending passages in the old books had to be obscured with black ink. Pictures of Japanese battleships and other military hardware were blotted out in similar fashion.

Demokurashii was to be instilled in the Japanese people as though none of them had heard of the concept before. This involved, among other things, the "three S's": sex, screen, and sport. Baseball was encouraged as an intrinsically democratic game. American tutors were concerned about the feudalistic relations between Japanese men and women, who never held hands, let alone kissed in public. Kissing scenes in prewar Hollywood movies had been censored in Japan. So the occupation authorities decreed that henceforth there should be kissing in Japanese films. The first movie to take the plunge was entitled *20-Year-Old Youth* and created a sensation. One zealous occupation officer had the smart idea that square dancing would be an ideal way to liberate Japanese from feudalism and introduced this novelty to some rural folks.

There was a great deal of idealism, as well as naïveté, in the American attempt to bring democracy to Japan. As always, idealism breeds hypocrisy. For even as the Japanese were lectured on their right to free speech, criticism of occupation policies was banned. Satirical cartoons of SCAP were forbidden. And SCAP officials were so keen to present the United States and its citizens as models of virtue and probity that unfavorable views were censored. *The Grapes of Wrath*, John Steinbeck's novel about American poverty, was banned, as were books and films about the bombings of Hiroshima and Nagasaki. Much as kissing, hand-holding, and dancing were to be encouraged among the Japanese, photographs of GIs fraternizing with local girls were out of bounds. However, since the right to free speech was part of the American way, mention of occupation censorship was also strictly forbidden.

The lessons of American culture were most effective when they were imparted on an unofficial and thus voluntary basis. After almost ten years of cultural deprivation and military propaganda, most Japanese were hungry for anything foreign and upbeat. During the war, "films about personal happiness" had been expressly forbidden in Japan. So Glenn Miller and Betty Grable probably did more for Japanese liberation than any number of high-minded lectures on *demokurashii*. Not since the late 1920s and early 1930s had there been such a taste for *ero guro nansensu*, the erotic, the grotesque, and the absurd: Strip shows were popular, as were pinup magazines with such exotic titles as *L'Amour, Liebe, Nightclub,* and *Neo-Riberal* (*sic*). Millions of people were hungry and homeless. Orphans were sleeping in the railway stations. But the big hit of 1948 was entitled "Tokyo Boogie-Woogie." It went something like this:

> *Tokyo Boogie-Woogie*
> *Rhythm. Wowie Wowie*
> *My heart goes pit-a-pat. Tick-a-tack.*
> *A song of the world. A happy song.*
> *Tokyo Boogie-Woogie.*

Despite temporary bans issued by puritanical officers of SCAP on "fraternization with indigenous personnel," the first Japanese to get close to the American forces were the "pan-pan girls," amateurs and professionals who "fraternized" with GIs in exchange for stockings, money, food, or simply a place to sleep. Loitering in the charred parks and swampy bomb craters of wrecked city centers, they dressed in cheap approximations of American fashions and mimicked the mannerisms of Hollywood stars. Envied and despised in equal measure, the pan-pan girls were among the pioneers of American commercial culture in postwar Japan—along with the children, who ran after every GI begging for chocolate and chewing gum, which were usually distributed with typical largesse from jeeps speeding through the ruins.

Intellectuals, disdainful of popular American culture, would turn to French literature for solace. A carefully cultivated air of nihilism was adopted by some of the more sophisticated men of letters. Marxism immediately made a comeback at the universities and in the coffee shops of

Tokyo and Kyoto. But in whatever form or guise, arts and entertainment flourished under the occupation, despite petty rules of censorship, which were in any case not comparable to the suffocating restraints of the militarist years. Japanese didn't have to be taught or encouraged to embrace intellectual and artistic freedom.

Culture was actually a bit of a red herring anyway. Japan's problems did not stem from the Kabuki theater or Mount Fuji. The main problem was the emperor-centered *kokutai*, the sacred national polity in whose cause civil liberties had been crushed.

Fanatical concern about the preservation of the *kokutai* is what prevented the wartime leadership, including Emperor Hirohito himself, from conceding defeat before Hiroshima and Nagasaki. Some Americans, especially the conservative experts on the Japanese mind, had argued that the Allies should give in on this point. Joseph Grew, for example, the prewar U.S. ambassador to Japan, wanted the Allies to guarantee the continuation of the imperial line. Others, often of a more liberal disposition, believed that this would compromise any effort to get at the roots of modern Japanese militarism. This same tension continued under MacArthur's administration, which was split between liberal supporters of Roosevelt's New Deal and hard right-wingers. Most of the New Dealers were, like MacArthur himself, full of ideals but relatively ignorant about Japan. The right-wingers thought they knew a bit more. The fact that some of the latter, such as General Charles Willoughby (born Weidenbach), head of the intelligence section, had German roots is most probably incidental.

After the Japanese surrender in 1945, the Japanese government was led for two months by Prince Higashikuni Naruhiko, an unimpressive nobleman with strong ties to

the imperial family. His deputy was Prince Konoe Fumimaro, who had been prime minister during the China war.
Both men still hoped that the *kokutai* would carry on much
as before, even without the Imperial Army. There would
have to be some reforms, of course, but they should be
slow and limited in scope. Higashikuni appointed some
peculiar advisers. The man put in charge of the spiritual
mobilization of the Japanese people, whose lack of spirit
was blamed for the nation's defeat, was Ishiwara Kanji, the
plotter in Manchuria. In September 1945, he was still making speeches about the coming clash between Asia and the
West. Another adviser was Kodama Yoshio, an uncouth
right-wing fixer who had made a fortune in occupied
China. In August 1945, Kodama was busy setting up brothels for the American troops, as well as finding ways to protect the old order. When SCAP decided in October to
abolish the legal restraints on free speech and civil rights,
Higashikuni decided that his time was up and resigned.
Ishiwara, rather to his own surprise, escaped being indicted
as a war criminal and died in 1949. Kodama was charged
with war crimes, spent some time in jail, but continued to
play a shady role in right-wing politics until the mid-
1970s, when he was exposed in a major corruption scandal.
  Right-wing ideologues, war criminals, and reactionary
princes were not the only ones who tried to protect the
kokutai. More important were the men identified by American diplomats as "moderates," such as Yoshida Shigeru, a
flowery Anglophile who had picked up some Churchillian
manerisms in the 1930s when he served as ambassador
in London. Regarded as a typical prewar liberal, Yoshida
was foreign minister in Higashikuni's cabinet and became
prime minister in 1946. In temperament and style, Yoshida
belonged to the Taisho period. The extreme militarism of

the late 1930s and early 1940s had been, in his view, an unfortunate but wholly untypical episode in Japan's development as a modern state. The best thing would be to revert to the kind of system that existed before it was hijacked by the military, when Japan was governed in a quasi-democratic manner by a paternalistic civilian elite. The imperial system would remain, of course, and a fully fledged American-style democracy would not be appropriate to Japan. However liberal he'd been before the war, in postwar terms, this made him a conservative.

Yoshida found allies for his conservative views in MacArthur's administration, but not among SCAP's New Dealers. A shrewd manipulator of American differences, Yoshida divided SCAP officials into "idealists" and "realists." SCAP himself was typically ambivalent. He encouraged such early measures as the dissolution of the *zaibatsu,* the abolition of the thought police, full voting rights for women, the release of communists and other political prisoners, the establishment of independent trade unions, and, most important, the promulgation of a new, liberal constitution. Japanese leftists and liberals greeted these reforms with delight. Yoshida and his fellow conservatives were not happy at all but were powerless to stop them. Concerning the emperor, however, there was a convergence of Japanese and American aims. SCAP's views on the emperor's future role were not the same as Yoshida's, let alone those of more right-wing Japanese, but he was just as keen to protect the throne.

This is well illustrated by a small but shabby example of occupation censorship. In 1946, the left-wing director Kamei Fumio made a documentary film entitled *The Japanese Tragedy.* Old newsreels, newspaper cuttings, and photographs were spliced together in a collage to expose the nature of Japanese wartime propaganda. The film includes several images of Hirohito, in and out of uniform, and the question of his war guilt is plainly addressed. *The Japanese Tragedy* passed the censors and was shown in a few provincial cinemas before its intended release in Tokyo. Suddenly, however, the U.S. censors banned the film after all. The reason for this turnabout was that Yoshida had objected to it and used his contacts with General Willoughby's staff to get SCAP to stop the film from being screened. Willoughby was an open admirer of General Franco; indeed, after his stint in Japan, he became his adviser. He also enjoyed excellent relations with Emperor Hirohito's court and was a regular guest at imperial duck shoots.

The reason given for the ban was that the film's "radical treatment" might "well provoke riots and disturbances." SCAP had used the same excuse for keeping the emperor on his throne. The Australians, the British, and the Soviets wanted to charge Hirohito with war crimes. MacArthur always maintained that Japan would be ungovernable without him. This fitted his idea of Japanese as childlike people who would run amok without imperial guidance, but was it really so? Members of Hirohito's family had expected him to abdicate and take moral responsibility for the war. Opinion polls taken at the time suggest that most Japanese would have gone along with this and perhaps even welcomed it. It was SCAP himself who insisted otherwise. Like the shoguns in pre-Meiji Japan, he wanted to use the emperor as a symbolic presence, a kind of shrine to legitimize his own authority. One reason Prime Minister Yoshida and other conservatives ended up agreeing to all SCAP's reforms was their fear that this shrine, and thus the last vestige of the *kokutai,* would be taken away before they could use it for themselves.

First, however, SCAP had to strip the throne of its political authority and religious mystique. This involved institutional and constitutional changes: Shinto ritual was to be separated from state affairs, and the emperor was to become a "symbol of national unity" instead of being a divine priest-king. It also involved a masterstroke of public relations. The transformation of the emperor was symbolized in one official photograph, taken when the emperor arrived for an audience with SCAP at the U.S. embassy in September 1945. MacArthur, in an open-necked shirt, his hands lodged easily in his hip pockets, towers over the diminutive monarch, standing stiffly at attention in his formal morning coat, his mouth slightly open. The photo was released to all the Japanese papers. You had to have been very obtuse to miss the true nature of U.S.-Japanese relations.

In January 1946, Hirohito, coached by his American tutors, renounced his divinity, much to the disgust of Japanese conservatives. One month later, Japan had a new draft constitution. It had not been an easy birth. To begin with, SCAP asked Japanese jurists to revise the old Meiji constitution. The jurists were distinguished "moderates," often, like Yoshida, with Anglophile reputations. But they were trained in the German legal tradition. American notions of popular sovereignty were strange to them. None of them really saw any point in changing the Meiji constitution. They tried to convince the Americans that the Meiji constitution was part of Japan's ancient tradition, which could not be replaced by a product of a very different civilization. There was talk of plants that grow only in certain types of soil. They appear to have lost sight of the fact that the Meiji constitution was largely Prussian in origin. In any case, they did little more than tinker with it. When their efforts were leaked to the press, most Japanese treated them with contempt. So much for ancient traditions.

After the Japanese jurists were dismissed, MacArthur instructed his government section chief, Courtney Whitney, who had been the general's lawyer before the war, to assemble a team of Americans to draft the constitution. They had a week to complete the task. The Americans, cloistered in the ballroom of SCAP's general headquarters, were young and inexperienced. Beate Sirota, a twenty-two-year-old Jewish woman born in Vienna, was in charge of social rights. To learn how these things were done, she borrowed copies of other constitutions from the library. The Soviet and the Weimar constitutions turned out to be the most useful. A young ensign, Richard Poole, was told to draft the provisions about the emperor's new status. It was he who turned the emperor from a human deity into a "symbol." Beate Sirota managed to secure special provisions on women's rights.

The translated version of the constitution reads awkwardly in parts, but it proved to be one of the most popular and durable products of the occupation. Conservatives such as Yoshida didn't like it, but they put up with it and later learned how to use it to their advantage. But there was one section of Japanese society, a small but at times vociferous and influential section, that positively hated it: the hard Right. They were unhappy about the emperor's new status as a mere symbol, but outraged by the most radical innovation, Article 9, which took away Japan's sovereign right to maintain its own armed forces and wage war. Even the young Richard Poole questioned the realism of constitutional pacifism, but he was quickly told that the instruction had come from the general himself. So that was that.

Alienating the hard Right was in any event not of great concern in 1946. Most Japanese were quite content never to have to fight another war. Besides, Article 9 allowed them to bask in the warm glow of moral satisfaction: the first pacifist nation in history. But this great symbol of early postwar idealism had the unintended consequence of perpetuating one of the main problems of the Meiji state. The Rescript for Soldiers and Sailors of 1882 mandated that the Imperial Armed Forces owed their loyalty to the emperor and not to the state. This lifted matters of war out of parliamentary politics to the more exalted but unaccountable level of the imperial throne. Since the United States would take care of Japan's military affairs from now on, the unaccountable throne had simply moved to Washington, D.C. This might have made many people, in Japan as well as outside, feel safer, but it did nothing to strengthen Japanese democracy in an area where it was really needed.

—

Reforming the Japanese mind also involved a history lesson. Punishment was not enough; the Japanese had to be shown clearly what they had done wrong. All over east Asia and Southeast Asia, Japanese who had carried out the holy war's dirty work were hanged or incarcerated, not always after fair or scrupulous trials. But the grand reckoning took place at the former headquarters of the Japanese army in Tokyo, the same place where the novelist Mishima Yukio would disembowel himself a couple of decades later. From May 1946 until November 1948, justices from eleven Allied nations, including the Soviet Union, sat in judgment of the generals, politicians, and diplomats who had waged war in the name of the emperor. They included the general in charge of the rape of Nanking, some of the men who plotted to take over Manchuria, the leaders who planned the attack on Pearl Harbor, the prime ministers and diplomats who prosecuted the war in China and Southeast Asia, a right-wing ideologue (who feigned madness and was excused), and the man who was the emperor's closest adviser. The only one missing from this sorry bunch was the emperor himself.

The International Military Tribunal for the Far East was modeled after the court at Nuremberg. As in Nuremberg, new laws against plotting and carrying out the invasion of other countries were applied retroactively, and justice was dispensed in the name of "civilization" by a bench that included one of Stalin's henchmen. Like the Germans, the Japanese were charged with crimes against humanity, a new category devised in response to the Nazi genocides. Parallels between the German and the Japanese wars were crudely drawn. The Nanking massacre, one of the most shocking episodes of the Japanese war, took on the symbolic weight of Auschwitz, even though the Japanese government had never had a policy of systematic genocide. The demoralized men staring blankly at their accusers in Tokyo were, on the whole, rather different from the Nazis in Nuremberg. Göring, Hess, Ribbentrop, Frank, and others had been part of a criminal regime that grabbed power in 1933. The defendants in Tokyo were in many cases highly educated gentlemen of the old civilian elite that had governed Japan before the war began. The others were military men.

There was no Japanese equivalent to the Nazi Party, or Hitler. The Japanese were guilty of many crimes, but they were committed in the name of the *kokutai*, with the emperor as its divine leader. Every soldier and sailor had received imperial instructions to "consider an order from your superior to be an order from Myself." But since

SCAP had decided that the emperor was innocent and had to be kept out of the trial, even as a witness, the Tokyo history lesson was given a mendacious and politically damaging twist. The "militarists" had to carry all the blame. They had led the emperor astray, just as they had misled the Japanese people. The fact that Hirohito had often been better informed than his generals was glossed over, as was the considerable popular enthusiasm, at least in the early stages of the war, for military adventures abroad. And if the man who had been formally responsible for everything was innocent, it was hard to see how those who thought they were following his sacred orders could be found guilty.

The trial was broadcast on Japanese radio and exhaustively reported in the press. But most people were too hungry to care about history lessons for very long. To be sure, news of the massacres in Nanking, Manila, and countless other places came as a shock, as did the evidence of official lying all through the war. Few ordinary citizens felt much sympathy for the class A war criminals. Most thought that they had got their just desserts. Since they had led Japan to a catastrophic defeat, they should take the consequences. But SCAP's protection of the throne had obscured the most important lesson of all—the questions of political responsibility, the nature of the *kokutai,* the link between imperial ideology and crimes against other Asians. If all Japanese, except for the militarists, were as innocent as their emperor, they were victims. And if the killing of civilians in China was a crime, then so were the bombings in Hiroshima and Nagasaki, or indeed Tokyo, Osaka, and all the other Japanese cities. In short, SCAP had let the Japanese off the hook.

Only once did the truth threaten to upset the carefully stage-managed trial. In December 1947, Tojo Hideki took the stand. Prime minister at the beginning of the war in the Pacific, General Tojo, with his round tortoiseshell glasses, shaved head, and buckteeth, was the favorite American caricature of the evil Japanese, the Fu Manchu, as it were, of Japanese militarism. People paid black market prices to watch his performance in the dock. Although he took personal responsibility for losing the war, unlike his colleagues, he made a dangerous slip. "None of us [Japanese]," he declared, "would dare act against the emperor's will." The cross-examination was cut short. Pressure was put on him to revise his testimony, and a week later Tojo dutifully stated that the emperor had always loved and wanted peace.

On December 22, 1948, a cold, gray day, seven of the Japanese defendants, including Tojo, were hanged at Sugamo prison after a simple meal of cold rice and sake. The prison was demolished in the 1970s, and on the place of the gallows arose a tall skyscraper named Sunshine Building. General Tojo is still remembered; he was depicted as the hero in a popular war movie in the 1990s. But the rest, Araki, Itagaki, Kido, and so on, are largely forgotten figures now. The Japanese who dwell on the Tokyo trials are the same ones who wish to revise Article 9: right-wing historians, journalists, and politicians who reject the notion that Japan was any more guilty than other nations involved in the war. They dismiss the history lesson that emerged from the trial as U.S. propaganda, which was subsequently, in their view, parroted by the Japanese Left.

———

The Japanese Left had its own reasons for resentment. In the beginning, when the New Dealers were in charge and "feudalism" was the main bugbear of SCAP's government section, socialists and communists were not only freed from prison but actively encouraged to help in the reforms. They did so with enthusiasm. Keen Japanese bureaucrats revised the labor laws, and for the first time in Japanese history, trade unions, often led by communists, were given real clout. Millions of workers joined up. Strikes and demonstrations were common. In some cases, workers took over the factories. On one occasion, they even threatened to storm the imperial palace. Marxist academics drew up blueprints for a planned economy. State intervention in the economy was one area where New Dealers, Japanese bureaucrats, and the Marxists saw eye to eye. In 1947 and 1948, Japan had its first socialist prime minister. One of the most sweeping reforms, encouraged by the Americans but planned and carried out by Japanese bureaucrats, was the redistribution of land from big landowners to their tenants. It was at once a progressive measure, applauded by the Left, and a way to avert the kind of rural unrest that was helping the communists in China. Poor tenant farmers, brutalized by their wretched lives, had been the harshest foot soldiers of Japan's holy war. Now a new class of rural smallholders was born, with the unintended consequence of helping the conservatives remain in office until this day.

Another thing that cannot have been intended was that SCAP reforms boosted Japanese bureaucrats at the expense of elected politicians. The newly created Ministry on International Trade and Industry (MITI) was put in charge of central economic planning. New Dealers were also convinced that private big business was largely to blame for Japanese imperialism. The solution, as they saw it, was to take these businesses out of the hands of the families that owned them. This task, too, was left up to the bureaucrats, the same bureaucrats, in fact, who had integrated the *zaibatsu* into the war economy, often against the private owners' wishes. Unwittingly, American left-wingers, because of their instinctive hostility to big business, were handing over more powers to the very institutions that helped to drive Japan toward war. As a result, politicians were reduced to being brokers between corporate and bureaucratic interests.

It is hard to be precise about the moment when the antifeudalist, reformist enterprise reversed its course and became a conservative crackdown on communism in all its alleged manifestations. U.S. bankers and business leaders had been dismayed by SCAP's reforms from the start. In 1947, SCAP felt the need to ban a general strike in February because of worries that the communists were wrecking the Japanese economy. With hyperinflation raging, there was indeed cause for alarm. Other measures soon followed: Civil servants were no longer allowed to strike. And the planned dissolution of private business combines was much reduced in scope. Yoshida and other conservatives were pleased to see that the "realists" in SCAP were beginning to prevail over the "idealists." But after all the initial encouragement, Japanese leftists felt betrayed by the Americans.

Two reasons help to explain this turn of events. First, with the Republicans in control of Congress in the late 1940s, Washington was no longer inclined to prop up the Japanese with U.S. taxpayers' money. And second, Mao's communists were close to victory in China. Hard-nosed grandees such as George Kennan believed that it was time to put democratic ideals to one side and concentrate on economic recovery. A tough banker by the name of Joseph

Dodge was dispatched to Tokyo in February 1949 to help bring down inflation and balance the budget. The "Dodge line" was that Japanese workers and consumers should make sacrifices for the national good. Export industry, guided by able bureaucrats and fed by the natural resources of Southeast Asia, would be the engine of Japan's revival as a fortress against communism. Homegrown leftists were dealt with in a "Red purge" of potential troublemakers in government, unions, and private enterprises.

SCAP, though never exactly a friend of the "Reds," was distressed, because he saw his control of Japanese affairs slipping. However, all this was sweet music to the ears of Japanese conservatives, who were now coming together nicely as a new elite—with some trusted old faces—made up of bureaucrats, politicians, and big-business leaders. This new elite was in many ways like the old elite in the 1920s, but without the unwelcome competition of power-hungry generals. Dodge's anti-inflationary measures put a lot of people out of work, which gave the Communist Party 10 percent of the vote in 1949, but Yoshida's Liberal Party still won the elections by a landslide.

The Korean War, which broke out the following year, provided just the kind of liftoff the Japanese economy needed. The *zaibatsu*, now reconstructed around big banks, supplied the unprepared American troops with everything they needed, for very stiff prices. Leftists, liberals, and pacifists, already embittered by the "reverse course," were especially disgusted to see Japan being drawn into another Asian conflict. The final blow was the emergence of an ersatz Japanese army in the form of a police reserve, which was forced upon the Japanese government—against SCAP's wishes—by Washington, even though it was in conflict with the pacifist constitution. But the economy was growing, and this mattered more in a hungry nation. The main casualty of the war, apart from millions of Koreans, was the career of the supreme commander himself. Despite his victory at Inchŏn, MacArthur's megalomania became too much for President Truman. When SCAP publicly stated his desire to take the war into China, if necessary with nuclear bombs, he was dismissed.

The reaction in Japan was extraordinary. Even as rightists and leftists nursed their grievances, the liberal *Asahi* newspaper thanked MacArthur for teaching the Japanese people "the merits of democracy and pacifism" and guiding them "with kindness along this bright path." It continued in a way designed to warm SCAP's paternal heart: "As if pleased with his own children growing up, he took pleasure in the Japanese people, yesterday's enemy, walking step by step towards democracy...." The emperor came to thank him for everything he had done. The general's route to Haneda airport was lined with hundreds of thousands of tearful Japanese citizens waving little paper flags. Children were let off from school. NHK radio played "Auld Lang Syne." Prime Minister Yoshida waved good-bye as the *Bataan,* the same plane that brought SCAP to Atsugi airdrome in 1945, took off from Japan for the last time.

Much of MacArthur's mission, despite reverse courses, had been an astounding success. His idealism was now enshrined, for better or worse, in the constitution. The Japanese had full suffrage, freedom of speech, and, in theory, the right to pursue happiness freely and without discrimination. Militarism seemed to be dead and buried, and with a parliamentary democracy, the dreams of many generations, from Sakamoto Ryoma to Fukuzawa Yukichi, from the People's Rights Movement activists to the postwar democrats, seemed finally to have come true. Yet SCAP's legacy had some profound defects. The price of pacifism is a total dependency on others to defend you. This has kept right-wing revanchism alive and polarized political opinion on the one thing where there should have been consensus: the constitution itself. The war crimes trials and the constitution also left the Japanese with unresolved questions about their monarchy and a troubled attitude toward their past. In one respect, at least, Japan had become a distorted mirror image of the nation that tried so hard to shape it: High ideals made the flaws all the more obvious.

7

1955 AND ALL THAT

On Christmas Eve 1948, a thin middle-aged man in a shabby khaki uniform and a peaked cap was released from Sugamo prison. His soft lips formed a toothy smile as he boarded an American jeep. Kishi Nobusuke had just spent three years in Sugamo jail as a class A war crimes suspect. He had been General Tojo's minister of commerce and industry when Japan attacked Pearl Harbor. Before that he had been the industrial czar of Manchukuo. He was in fact the nearest Japanese equivalent to Albert Speer. His wartime responsibilities ranged from munitions to slave labor. If the war had been fought by soldiers, their conquests had been administered by people like him.

Many a postwar friendship was kindled or strengthened in Sugamo. Kishi's cellmate was Sasakawa Ryoichi, the leader of a small fascist party in the 1930s and a notorious racketeer in occupied China. He expanded his fortune after the war in various more or less opaque ways, which included a huge gambling enterprise. Wartime connections and a great deal of shady money made him a formidable backroom operator in postwar conservative politics. Sasakawa was released the same day as Kishi. Less than ten years later, Kishi would be prime minister of Japan.

In 1948, however, Yoshida Shigeru was still in charge. Though both moved in the same high-flown circles, Kishi and Yoshida did not like each other. Yoshida, born in Tosa, the son of a People's Rights Movement activist, was a genuine conservative compared to Kishi, a Choshu man, proud of his provincial samurai ancestry and a typical exponent of the more zealous Japanese Right. Kishi had more silky charm than the gruff Yoshida, who is still remembered in Japan for having called a socialist MP a "damned fool" in parliament. But from the time he entered Tokyo Imperial University to the end of his long career, Kishi's instincts were always on the opposite side of liberalism. As a young man, he admired Kita Ikki, the national socialist agitator behind the 1936 military rebellion. In the constitutional debates between Minobe and his rightist enemies, Kishi took the ultranationalist view. In Manchukuo, he was close to General Tojo and the Kwantung army. In 1939, he was in favor of strengthening the ties with Nazi Germany. In the struggles between businessmen and the military, he took the latter side. And in Sugamo prison, he still believed Japan had fought "a just war."

Even though Kishi became a defender of democracy after the war, his politics were in some ways remarkably consistent. Before and during the war, he described himself as a national socialist: authoritarian, nationalistic, and socialist in the sense of seeing a planned economy as the right way to strengthen the nation and spread its wealth. He was never a believer in laissez-faire, or liberal Anglo-Saxon-style capitalism. In 1953, Kishi spoke out against policies of "the 'let-alone' type." What was needed, instead, was centralized industrial planning that "should be carefully worked out—like the Russian five-year plans." Just before making this statement, he had been on a trip to West Germany, where he had had a pleasant encounter with his old colleague, the former Nazi economics minister Hjalmar Schacht. Kishi's economic ideas were and would remain very close to the mainstream of Japanese thinking.

———

In their battles for the conservative leadership, Kishi encouraged the common perception of Yoshida as a SCAP toady, an American boy, a good Jap who did as he was told.

This was not entirely fair. In 1951, just as MacArthur was flying back to the United States, John Foster Dulles was on his way to Tokyo as a special envoy to conclude a peace treaty with the Japanese. They conferred on the radio in midflight. Dulles was under instructions to put pressure on Japan to build a serious army. Yoshida—and SCAP—had been fighting Washington on this issue for some years already. In 1948, MacArthur argued that such a move would be contrary to his principles and place the Americans "in a ridiculous light before the Japanese people." When he was instructed to make the Japanese build a national police reserve, he still spoke of Japan as "the Switzerland of the Pacific" and stalled. In 1950, with the Korean War, further resistance was futile, and seventy-five thousand Japanese "police officers," dressed in cast-off U.S. uniforms, were given machine guns, tanks, and bazookas. Yoshida pretended that these Imperial Army veterans weren't real soldiers. They were deployed around industrial areas to crack down on communist agitation. But soon they were given more extensive hardware and renamed the Japanese Self-Defense Forces.

Dulles demanded more. He wanted 350,000 Japanese under arms. Yoshida resisted such a clear breach of the peace constitution. It would cause huge upheavals, he warned, not just in Japan but all over Asia. To make his point, Yoshida secretly encouraged socialists to demonstrate in front of his office. He held the Japanese Self-Defense Forces to seventy-five thousand. In the end a compromise was reached, which Yoshida could claim as a victory of sorts. The United States would have unlimited access for an indefinite period to Japanese territory for military bases. Okinawa would become a huge military installation under U.S. government administration. Japan promised in time to assume responsibility for its own defense. When was not specified. Until that fine day, the United States would take care of Japanese security, and Japan was free to pour all its energy into government-directed industrial growth. In December 1951, in San Francisco, a peace treaty and a security treaty were signed simultaneously. Sovereignty was regained, up to a point. The constitutional problem was no longer mentioned. The Yoshida deal was done.

The end of the occupation meant that Japanese were free at last to vent their frustrations. Stoked by leftist intellectuals, the Communist Party, and union leaders, students and workers staged massive demonstrations against the security treaty on May Day 1952. Crowds charged the police on the imperial palace plaza. The police responded with guns, tear gas, and baton charges. Two people were killed on this occasion, and many people got badly beaten up or trampled in the chaos. This did nothing to dampen the anger of Japanese liberals and leftists. Often starry-eyed about the Soviet Union and filled with a kind of guilt-ridden solidarity with the Chinese communists, the Left wanted out of any security arrangement with the United States. This time, to atone for its historic error of trying to be a Western-style imperialist power, Japan should be on the side of its Asian neighbors. It would never go to war with them again. That, after all, is what the renunciation of using military force meant. For the Japanese Left, Article 9 of General MacArthur's constitution had become holy writ.

Rightists such as Kishi were eager to take the American side in the cold war, but they argued for constitutional revision, both of Article 9 and Article 1, concerning the emperor's new, secular status. Pragmatic conservatives such as Yoshida were happy to let the Americans fight the communists while Japan got on with its own business, and hoped the constitutional debate would simply go away. Well, it would and it wouldn't. Two-thirds of the Diet was needed to revise the constitution, and since this was an unlikely prospect, resentments boiled over in riots, polemics about Japan's wartime history, textbook controversies, anti-American diatribes, and sound trucks running around the streets with uniformed thugs spouting right-wing revanchism.

The early 1950s were a golden age for Japanese cinema, with masterpieces by Ozu, Mizoguchi, and Kurosawa. But film was also a perfect vehicle for right- and left-wing anti-Americanism. On the right were such movies as *Battleship Yamato* and *Eagle of the Pacific*, celebrating the spirit of the Imperial Navy and its brave and blameless admirals. On the left were such cinematic tracts as *Hiroshima*, sponsored by the radical Teachers Union, which portrayed the atom bombing as an act of racism. It ends with American tourists coming to Hiroshima to collect souvenir bones of the victims. Just as popular were semipornographic films about the rapacious behavior of GIs around the military bases. Base movies were a vibrant subgenre of the blossoming sex industry. Some of these fantasies were remarkable for their viciousness. The patriotic heroine of one popular comic book, later made into a film, was a diseased Japanese whore who slept with as many Americans as she could to infect the U.S. Army with syphilis. The same charming theme was later taken up in a burlesque show in Tokyo, entitled *The Tachikawa Base: Ten Solid Years of Rape.*

Even though Hiroshima and Nagasaki were the prime symbols of anti-American pacifism, the Japanese Left did not play down Japanese war crimes. On the contrary, the war was discussed more critically in Japan during the

1950s than in Germany, sometimes with dire consequences. Army veterans who wrote a confessional account
of their brutal deeds in China were denounced as communists, and their publisher, threatened by right-wing thugs,
withdrew the book. But the correct line in left-wing intellectual circles and the influential Teachers Union was
heavy with Marxist dogma: The Chinese communists had
been brave freedom fighters in a war of liberation against
Japanese capitalist imperialism and "the emperor system."
Hiroshima should have turned Japan into a beacon of
peace. The new enemy in Asia was American imperialism
and its Japanese running dogs.

The Right, led by Kishi, still maintained that Japan's war
had been just. This issue began to replace, as a kind of substitute, the necessary political debate on the constitution.
Whenever the Left used the barbarity of Japan's war record
as an argument for constitutional pacifism, the Right would
deny that Japan had done anything wrong, or at least anything more wrong than other nations in wartime. The rows
over textbooks, which continue to this day, between the
Teachers Union and the conservative Ministry of Education, are really about this. Article 9, described in 1953
by Vice President Richard Nixon as "an honest mistake,"
had left the Japanese bitterly divided over their most recent history for essentially nonhistorical reasons. A salient
aspect of the endless polemics about the war in Japan's
popular press is the conspicuous lack of participation by
professional historians, who tended to confine their writing
to strictly academic channels.

———

The Left might have been more successful in postwar
Japan if it had been less dogmatic and prone to tear itself
apart. After the riots in 1952, the communists began to fall

out of favor. The Communist Party had tried to gather the marginal and disadvantaged around the Red banner: Koreans, outcasts, and day laborers. But violent purges and the intolerance of dissent made the Communist Party itself more and more marginal. The socialists, however, divided in a right and left wing, still occupied about one-third of the lower house seats, sometimes more, sometimes less. They were backed by the largest trade union, which was led by leftist hard-liners and still had considerable power. The conservatives were split between the Democrat Party and the Liberal Party, led by Yoshida.

For a moment, in 1955, it looked as though the Socialist Party might have a chance. The right and left wings made peace and merged into one Japan Socialist Party (JSP). But this galvanized the Liberals and Democrats, who, after a spate of mutual calumny and backstabbing, formed the Liberal Democrat Party (LDP). The architect of the merger was Kishi, and big business was the force that drove it. The first LDP leader was Hatoyama Ichiro, another veteran of the old *kokutai* elite who had been purged by SCAP for his suppression of free speech in the 1930s. This new alignment of parties became known as the "1955 System."

In December 1955, a young radical student at Kyoto University, soon to become a world-famous film director, wrote the following sentence in his diary: "Ten years after the war it looks superficially as if democratic forces have suffered a setback. But in fact they have progressed. The time of unruly romanticism has come to an end. The masses have got their foothold now and we enter a time of realism." A few years on, Oshima Nagisa would be deeply disillusioned.

The Japan Socialist Party started off with a self-inflicted handicap. As a result of the merger, the left wing dominated the party leadership. Despite the popularity of pacifism in Japan, the JSP's aim to lead the workers' revolution against capitalism in Asia hardly matched the more modest aspirations of most Japanese. The LDP, on the other hand, quickly made the 1955 System into the LDP System. With the help of big business, Washington, senior bureaucrats, and an electoral system that favored the conservative rural areas, the LDP built up a formidable political machine. It was founded on money: money from construction companies, crime syndicates, industrial corporations, CIA slush funds, and trading companies, sluiced through a network of pork barrels, managed by party factions whose members could expect tenure in the Diet as long as the money kept flowing to their constituents. The factions were formed around powerful bosses, who were rotated as party leaders and prime ministers, so that everyone had a chance to feed at the trough. To operate smoothly, the LDP System relied on fixers behind the scenes, which is where old racketeers such as Sasakawa Ryoichi and Kodama Yoshio came in. Every new LDP prime minister vowed to abolish the factions. None of them did. The socialists did not get another chance to govern for forty years, and even then they did not last long.

So Oshima Nagisa, the film director, was right. A new age was at hand, but not the one he had envisaged. In 1956, Japanese were mesmerized by a new slogan: "The Post-War is Over." It was the first sentence of the Economic White Paper, which set the scene for almost forty years of breakneck economic growth. Although it would later become common among Japanese intellectuals and politicians to attribute economic success to ancient Japanese virtues—obedience, self-sacrifice, hard work—or aspects of the "national character"—technical dexterity, superior sensitivity, group consciousness—the postwar boom had American as well as Japanese fathers: Douglas MacArthur and Joseph Dodge had had almost as much to do with it as the wartime bureaucrats and conservative politicians, who managed a remarkably smooth transition from the prewar *kokutai* to the LDP System.

———

There was to be another upheaval, however, another spasm of the fading influence of the radical Left. When Kishi became prime minister in 1957, he was keen to settle the unresolved constitutional problem once and for all. To restore Japan's status as an independent sovereign power, both the constitution and the security treaty needed to be revised. The security treaty, which gave the United States a free hand on Japanese soil, reminded many Japanese, on the Right and the Left, of the unequal treaties in the 1860s. U.S. bases were constantly being attacked by irate mobs. Kishi wanted the revisions because he was a nationalist, but also because he wished to see a system of two conservative parties holding each other in check. He believed that as long as there was no basic agreement over the constitution and Japan was humiliated by an unequal treaty, politics would continue to be a struggle between a radicalized Left and one conservative party, easily corrupted by its monopoly on power. For all his past sins, Kishi's analysis would prove to be correct.

To smooth the way toward a more assertive Japan, Kishi first went on a grueling tour of Southeast Asia, where he apologized for the atrocities committed by Japanese troops. He also played golf in Washington with President Eisenhower. Still, Kishi's attempts to change the constitution came to nothing. But he tried hard to get the cooperation of leftists as well as conservatives for his security treaty revisions. The problem was that few people really trusted the old apparatchik. A botched attempt to give the police more sweeping powers resulted in riots outside the Diet building. Then he introduced "moral education" in schools, a measure that smacked of prewar patriotic propaganda. Not surprisingly, the socialists changed their mind about the treaty revisions and decided to oppose him all the way.

The deal he was promised in Washington was a minor improvement. The Japanese would be "consulted" in future about U.S. deployments of troops and equipment on their territory. Eisenhower would seal the new deal with a visit to Tokyo. It was something, but not enough. By the end of 1959, radical students were rushing toward the Diet and pissing on its doors. First tens of thousands, then hundreds of thousands joined the demonstrations. Police barricades were crushed. The liberal newspapers, stirred by pacifist patriotism and their loathing of Kishi, backed opposition to the security treaty. A young girl was trampled to death in a police charge. Soon almost a million people were in the streets, screaming—in English—"Yankee go home!"

The Socialist Party chairman, Asanuma Inejiro, called "American imperialism" the "common enemy of the Japanese and Chinese peoples." In a replay of prewar Japanese politics, he was stabbed to death by a right-wing fanatic. President Eisenhower's envoy was mobbed in his car on the way from the airport. Despite the promise of gangsters, organized by the old fixer Kodama Yoshio, to help the police guard his route, Eisenhower's visit to Japan had to be called off. For a moment it looked as if revolution might be at hand. All the hatred and distrust of the old order, and the United States, which was blamed, not without reason, for supporting it, gathered like a storm in the streets of Tokyo.

Kishi toyed with the idea of calling for the Japanese Self-Defense Forces, but fortunately he thought better of it.

In May 1960, there was almost as much mayhem inside the Diet itself. Ratification of the treaty in the lower house was boycotted by the socialists, first by blocking the debate in various ways, then by locking up the Diet Speaker in his office. The Speaker, who had been General Tojo's defense counsel at the Tokyo war crimes trials, ordered riot police to come in and release him. Under police protection, after midnight, the LDP forced a vote to ratify the treaty without a JSP member in sight. Kishi had won, but only just. He knew he had to resign. An attempt was made to kill him. His career, so spectacularly revived after the war, was over—in public, that is; behind the scenes he continued to be a formidable puppet player.

If the public Kishi was a spent force, so was the radical Left. There was a bloody strike in 1960, lasting many months, of coal miners who had lost their jobs when the government decided to meet Japan's energy needs with oil. In the late 1960s and 1970s, large numbers of students protested against the Vietnam War, but to no considerable effect. As would be the case in Germany and Italy, the radical Left splintered into murderous factions, whose members would hijack planes and plant bombs to promote the world revolution, but there would never be anything on the scale of 1960 again. After the hated Kishi had played his part as a lightning rod for popular frustrations, he was replaced by a dull financial bureaucrat, a Yoshida protégé named Ikeda Hayato. Ikeda did not solve Japan's constitutional problems, either. But he dealt with them by leaving them alone. He had found another way to dampen discord and appease discontent.

In 1958, Kishi had brought Ikeda into his cabinet as

minister of trade and industry. Ikeda's ministry, MITI, was the successor of Kishi's old Ministry of Commerce and Industry, which became the Ministry of Munitions during the war. MITI was at the heart of Japan's postwar economic expansion. Picking up on the idea of a well-known labor economist, Ikeda promised to make all Japanese richer. His Plan to Double Individual Income, published in December 1960, was a deliberate move to take people's minds off constitutional issues. Money, more evenly spread, would buy off the moderate wing of the Japan Socialist Party. Money, it was hoped, would make people forget about politics altogether. Stability and prosperity were guaranteed in the paternal LDP state by the competent technocrats who would guide the Japanese economy for the good of the nation. This was the essence of the Ikeda deal.

The disruptive leftist unions were either intimidated by criminal gangs or undermined by a new system of private company unions, which promised to take care of their workers, as though they were the children of corporate families. The largest companies offered their employees the security of lifetime employment in exchange for absolute loyalty. All these arrangements, often described as ancient Japanese traditions, were actually part of the Ikeda deal. Another part was a program of relentless construction, which turned Japanese cities but especially the countryside into a nationwide building site for ever more roads, bridges, and dams. This was good for the construction business and its gangster affiliates. It was good for ministries in charge of construction and agricultural development. It was good for Japanese industry. It was good for politicians who brought business to rural constituencies. So it was good for the LDP, whose coffers were filled with bribes and kickbacks that accrued to every new building project.

During the 1960s, Japan's GNP grew at an annual rate of 10.6 percent in real terms. This had the desired effect. The rifts that threatened to tear the country apart were now visible only on the fringes: right-wing thugs still flew the old battle flags and blared military marches from their sound trucks, and the most radical students tore one another to pieces in murderous purges. But most Japanese were politically stupefied by the new era of national prosperity. Pride swelled as a virtual replica of the Eiffel Tower went up in Tokyo, except that this one was higher. In 1964, the first bullet train whooshed from Tokyo to Osaka in three and a half hours. And the world came to Tokyo for the Olympic Games. For a moment, at long last, the Japanese could feel at peace with themselves and the world.

His task accomplished, Ikeda died in that same Olympic year. Another Yoshida protégé, Sato Eisaku, replaced him. Sato was Kishi Nobusuke's younger brother. He, too, sprinkled sleep, like the political sandman, over the issues most likely to cause controversy in Japan. His approach to foreign policy was simple. Historically, he said, "whenever Japan took a path counter to the United States, the country suffered; and whenever the two countries worked together closely, Japan prospered. My policy therefore, was to cooperate fully with the United States to ensure peace in the world." Sato promised peace, and more peace. And for this he was awarded the Nobel Peace Prize in 1972.

Epilogue:
The End of the Postwar

Is this, then, the end of the modern Japanese story? Of course not. But it is the end of the story I set myself to tell. A great deal has happened in Japan since 1964: governments brought down by corruption scandals; the death of Emperor Hirohito and the beginning of a new reign, called Heisei; a bubble economy that made it look as if Japan were about to consume the world; a poison gas attack on Tokyo by religious terrorists; the collapse of the bubble economy. And much else besides. But the postwar order, as it was constructed during the U.S. occupation and consolidated in 1955, is still intact. There are cracks in its foundation, and the timbers are showing signs of rot, but the edifice stands. Until it comes crashing down, 1964 is as good a time as any to mark the end of the rise and fall and rise of modern Japan.

There were moments when it looked as if real change were on the way. The winter of 1976 was such a time of high drama. I had come to Tokyo the year before as a student. Small traces of the war were still visible then. Veterans without arms or legs, dressed in white kimonos, sat outside the railway stations, playing sad wartime tunes on their keening accordions. They were visible, yet the people rushing past, a little too quickly, perhaps, appeared not to notice them, as though their haunting presence were just a chill in the balmy air of rising prosperity.

In front of Shinjuku station, the favored spot in the 1960s of student demos and theatrical "happenings," I watched people toss peanuts at a crude caricature of Tanaka Kakuei, the disgraced former prime minister. "Peanuts" was the term used by middlemen who collected cash from the Lockheed Corporation to be distributed among Japanese politicians, including Tanaka, in exchange for landing an aircraft deal. The main broker was Kodama Yoshio, the wartime racketeer who was in prison with Kishi Nobusuke. When news of this latest scandal broke, a young porno movie actor crashed his light plane into the Lockheed office in Tokyo as an act of protest against capitalist corruption. He wore the uniform of a kamikaze fighter. His last words were "Long live the emperor!" Thus does farce echo the tragedies of history.

Tanaka had already resigned as prime minister two years before for what the Japanese media termed his "money politics," yet he was astonished to be indicted for taking bribes. Indeed, he felt it as a stab in the back. Corruption, after all, had become a normal part of Japanese politics. It was the only way to get things done. Tanaka had simply outspent his rivals and got more things done. He was ousted in the end, not by investigative journalists, as many thought, but by his old rival Fukuda Takeo, a cunning ex-bureaucrat whose career, like Kishi Nobusuke's, began in Manchuria. Members of Fukuda's faction had leaked details of the case to the press. Having Tanaka brought down and kicked out of the LDP was Fukuda's revenge for Tanaka's attempt to usurp the LDP System. Even so, Fukuda could not destroy Tanaka's influence. Tanaka's faction continued to control the LDP for many years after the boss had left to become an independent lawmaker.

Tanaka was the consummate political populist, all glad hands and can-do, and Fukuda was the typical political bureaucrat. Since Ikeda made his pact with the Japanese people to smother politics with technocratic largesse, bureaucrats had dominated the LDP. They set the policies, wrote the parliamentary speeches for cabinet ministers, and took their places in the LDP hierarchy upon retirement from their ministries. The politicians' job was to work the pork barrels to make sure the LDP stayed in power. Factional rivalry inside the LDP ensured that no politician ever got above his station and ended up controlling the system. However, through a combination of political genius and pork barreling on a stupendous scale, Tanaka came closest to doing just that. His patronage had put so many people in his debt that this son of a rural cattle dealer who had not even completed high school almost managed to crack the bureaucratic dominance. For the first time in recent history, politicians were telling bureaucrats what to do. The result was that Tanaka made Japan vastly richer, and also vastly more corrupt.

To be a populist is not to be a democratic reformer. Tanaka never tried to reform the LDP System. He manipulated it to create wealth and jobs for the largest possible number of people. Tanaka's background was in construction. He married the daughter of his construction boss. Construction funded his political career. Tanaka promised to turn the whole Japanese archipelago into a construction site. Even when his influence waned after his stroke in 1985, the building program, and the resulting cash flow that kept the LDP afloat, continued with monotonous relentlessness: more roads, more bridges, more dams, more conference centers, more airports, more *pachinko* (pinball) parlors, more museums, more town halls, more hotels, tunnels, theme parks, and industrial zones. Many of these projects were useful—indeed, much needed. Many were not.

Japan is now full of unnecessary tunnels, roads that go no-where, lifeless rivers, bridges that nobody crosses, half-empty museums, and theme parks that few care to visit. These are the unlovely monuments of the Ikeda deal and Tanaka's money politics.

In terms of brute financial power, however, Tanaka's legacy was a fantastic success. In the 1980s, Tokyo yuppies ate gold leaf. With a prime piece of Japanese real estate, you could have bought yourself a small country. Japanese au-thors wrote books crowing about the coming "Japanese century": Today Tokyo, tomorrow the world! Foreigners wrote books about the coming war with Japan, or the all-conquering yen, or the unstoppable Japanese system, which could be countered only by equally combative in-dustrial policies of our own. Western businessmen read seventeenth-century tracts about samurai strategies. Books on Japanese management techniques became instant best-sellers. It seemed as though the great Japanese bonanza would never end.

Yet there was a sense among many Japanese of some-thing missing in their rich and increasingly ugly country. It was not for nothing that the leaders of Aum Shinrikyo, the quasi-Buddhist cult, which tried to commit mass mur-der in 1995 by spreading sarin gas in the Tokyo subways, were men and women of the highest education. Many of them were scientists or trained for the technocratic bu-reaucracy. They were the heirs of the Ikeda deal, and in the absence of political responsibility for the here and now, they filled their heads with murderous spiritual utopianism. The group aimed for a huge conflagration, a spectacular destruction of what they saw as a meaningless society. A wonderful new world would rise from the ashes of postwar affluence.

In the 1980s, conservative politicians and their intellectual supporters had also begun to fret about the lack of
values in modern Japan. The young, especially, softened by
the good life, seemed shiftless and lacking direction. Nakasone Yasuhiro, an ex–naval officer and member of the
Tanaka faction, tried to promote a new nationalism when
he became prime minister in the mid-1980s. In fact, the
propaganda associated with his period in office sounded
much like the old nationalism: the virtues of a monoracial
state, respect for the imperial institution, the uniqueness of
the Japanese spirit. Some of this was meant as an antidote
to the leftist dogmas cranked out for years by the Teachers
Union and Marxist intellectuals. Partly it was a ham-fisted
attempt to give meaning to a nation whose only political
aim was to expand its economic might. But nationalist
musing about the essence of Japaneseness was mainly a
poor substitute for political debate.

Nakasone's nationalism was little more than hollow
bluster anyway. It did not even have the political energy of
Kishi's attempts to revise the constitution. Nakasone may
have sounded at times like a wartime patriot, but he also
called Japan an unsinkable aircraft carrier for the United
States. No amount of nationalist rhetoric could change the
skewed nature of U.S.-Japanese relations. The Gulf War in
1991, fought partly to safeguard Japan's own oil supplies,
made this painfully apparent: The Japanese could only
look on, unable to help in a crisis that directly concerned
them. Japan's only role was to pay the United States and its
allies a huge amount of money, too late, and for scant
thanks. It was not just Japanese nationalists who felt a sense
of humiliation.

Two years after the Gulf War, the LDP, racked by more
corruption scandals and the defection of some powerful

politicians, lost an election. For a short while, it looked as though the LDP System might finally come to an end. Perhaps a new government formed by opposition parties could make the necessary reforms to inject life into Japan's blocked political system. One of the leading LDP defectors, a veteran pork barrel operator named Ozawa Ichiro, even talked of revising the constitution, to make Japan, as he put it, "a normal country." It was high time, he argued, that Japanese became individuals, prepared to take risks and stand up for themselves. Constitutional change would enable Japan to play a more independent role in the world. And revising the electoral system, skewed for so long in favor of the decreasing rural population, would lead to a robust two-party system, which would end the dominance of the LDP.

It turned out to be another false dawn. The electoral changes did not go far enough to make a difference. The opposition leaders wasted their energies fighting among themselves. Outside the LDP, Ozawa was unable to spread enough money around to get things done and keep his party members happy. In 1994, the LDP was back in power in coalition with, of all parties, the socialists. By 1997, Ozawa and his fellow rebels against the LDP were finished.

Yet something did change, not through political will, but through economic circumstances: The great bonanza ended in a massive stock market crash. Real estate prices tumbled, banks went under, and the Japanese bubble quickly seemed as fantastic in retrospect as tulip mania in seventeenth-century Amsterdam. Japanese triumphalists and Western alarmists were stunned into uncharacteristic silence. This did not bring down the LDP System, to be sure, but it more or less killed people's trust in it. The bureaucratic

elite lost much of its prestige. From trusted and safe guar-
antors of stability and growth, they came to be seen as arrogant blunderers out of touch with reality. The LDP still
rules, but faute de mieux, and no longer alone. It has to
share its power with other parties, such as the Komeito,
linked to a right-wing Buddhist organization. And for the
first time since the 1950s, even the highly educated salary-
men in the senior ranks of large corporations can no longer
be sure of a lifetime job. You see them in libraries, coffee
shops, and railway stations, men in neat blue suits reading
newspapers, pretending to work, but in fact cast adrift in a
society that is slowly unraveling. The economic crash has
not made many Japanese destitute, not yet. Fifty years of
high-speed growth created huge reserves of wealth. But
the Ikeda deal is over.

Even Tokyo, normally the most boisterous of capitals,
appears to be strangely subdued, as though people are
sunk into contemplation over what could possibly have
gone wrong. The prime minister, as I write these lines, is
Koizumi Junichiro, who became a media star in 2001 because of his plain speaking, his youthful appearance, and
his promises of radical reforms. Like all his predecessors,
he said he would abolish the party factions and curb bureaucratic interference. Under him, the corrupt old system
of kickbacks, out-of-control construction, and unaccountable budgets would be brought to heel. People hoped that
he might be the Japanese Gorbachev, the reformer who
brings down the system. It didn't happen. And public cyni-
cism toward the politics and politicians grows by the day.
In a young democracy, this is always ominous. Combined
with frustrated nationalism and economic despair, it could
nudge Japan once more into illiberal directions.

People talk of the current governor of Tokyo, Ishihara

Shintaro, as the man to watch. Some speak of him with desperate hope, as though he represented the last throw of the dice, and some with fear and loathing. Ishihara made his name as a popular novelist in the 1950s. Like Koizumi, he is admired for his telegenic looks and his outspoken views, which are publicized in an endless stream of books, videos, magazines, and TV talk shows. Like other populists before him, Ishihara, too, has voiced his discontent with the bureaucratic grip on the LDP System. His most famous novel, about rich teenage rebels, came out in 1955, the year the LDP was founded and one year before the Economic White Paper announced the end of the postwar. Ishihara's message since those days has barely wavered. He blames the United States for creating an effete and spiritually vapid nation. Japan, in his view, fought a just war, and he believes it is high time for postwar Japan to cut its umbilical cord with Washington and resume its position as the dominant power in Asia.

This, too, may be only so much bluster, an expression of frustration, and the lingering humiliation of wartime defeat. But it is not only people of his own generation who respond to Ishihara's emotional nationalism. It appeals to young people, too, the result, I think, of an intellectual culture stunted by dogmas of the Left and the Right. It is also the result of a political establishment that deliberately stifled public debate by opting for a monomaniacal concentration on economic growth. And it is the result of an infantile dependency on the United States. Until these problems are resolved, the postwar will not be over.

But how to resolve them? This is where the story goes back to the beginning, to the time when Japan first confronted the force of the West, the time when, in the opinion of some, the long war with the West began. I am writing in Tokyo, in the early spring of 2002. And I think of the number of times in the last few weeks when Japanese told me, in all seriousness, that they wished the black ships would come round once again, to unblock the political system. Only foreign pressure, they say, can cut the knots that tether this insular society to the old ways that no longer function. I can see what they mean, but I look forward, nonetheless, to the day when Japanese free themselves and can finally bid the black ships farewell, because they no longer need them.

GLOSSARY

Shogun: Literally it means "general." The shoguns were the military rulers of Japan. Between 1603 and 1867, the shoguns were from the same Tokugawa family. The time of their rule is called the Tokugawa or Edo period.

Edo: The name of the city where the Tokugawa shoguns resided. After 1867 and the end of Tokugawa rule, it was renamed Tokyo and became the capital of modern Japan.

Bakufu: The name of the shogun's government, or shogunate.

Samurai: The warrior caste. Samurai ranked from the shogun down to the lowliest retainer. Barred from engaging in trade, which was beneath them, the samurai were mostly poorly paid government servants. In times of peace, many of them were out of work. But they were the only caste allowed to bear arms or to commit ritual suicide.

Rangaku: Dutch learning. Since the early Tokugawa period, Dutch merchants were the only Europeans allowed to live in Japan. By learning Dutch, Japanese scholars were able to get access to European scientific knowledge.

Satsuma: The feudal domain located in what is now Kyushu prefecture. Satsuma was one of the three domains whose samurai clans rebelled against Tokugawa rule. It produced many prominent figures of the Meiji period, such as the statesman Okubo Toshimichi. Another Satsuma hero was Saigo Takamori, who led disaffected samurai in a revolt against the new government in Tokyo.

Choshu: The domain at the southwestern tip of the main island of Honshu. Choshu samurai rebelled against the Tokugawa rulers as allies, and sometimes as rivals, of the

Satsuma warriors. Ito Hirobumi, the great Meiji statesman, was a son of Choshu, as was the architect of the modern Imperial Army, Yamagata Aritomo.

Tosa: The poorest and most liberal-minded of the three rebellious domains. It lay in the southern part of the island of Shikoku. The most famous Tosa figure was Sakamoto Ryoma, the rural swordsman, who ended up drafting the Meiji constitution.

Bakumatsu: The last years of the Tokugawa *bakufu,* when Japan became a dangerous place full of intrigues, violent revolts, roaming swordsmen, and blood-soaked Kabuki plays.

Meiji Restoration: The revolt against Tokugawa rule, which established a new government in Tokyo, where the emperor now resided in the shogun's old castle. Meiji is the name for the period of the emperor's reign immediately after the restoration.

Bunmei Kaika: "Civilization and Enlightenment." The main slogan of the Meiji period, during which Japan attempted to become a modern nation in the European mold.

Fukoku Kyohei: "Strong Army, Rich Nation." The other Meiji-period slogan, a variation of "Civilization and Enlightenment" with a stress on military and economic might.

Diet: Parliament. Often used in the English language for parliamentary institutions outside Britain.

Taisho: The reign of the Meiji emperor's son, Yoshihito. It lasted officially from 1912 to 1926, but Yoshihito's son, Hirohito, had to step in as regent in 1922, because his father was no longer capable of carrying out his duties.

Kokutai: Polity. A semimystical idea of the Japanese nation, conceived as an authoritarian family state, ruled by the divine emperor. The "essence" of this sacred polity was laid down in the *Kokutai no Hongi,* or *Fundamentals of the National Polity,* published by the Ministry of Education in 1937.

Kodoha: The Imperial Way faction. In the late 1920s, a group of mostly young army officers and their intellectual mentors developed a revolutionary program that sought to rid Japan of noxious Western influences such as liberalism, individualism, and capitalism. Instead, they wanted to conquer the world through the Japanese spirit, personified by the divine emperor, whose absolute rule would be "restored." In February 1936, the Imperial Way tried to realize its ideals in a failed coup d'état.

Toseiha: The Control faction. This was the rival faction in the armed forces. Though its members did not necessarily disagree with the goals of the Imperial Way radicals, they favored a more disciplined approach. After crushing the attempted coup in 1936, the Control faction dominated military policy.

Zaibatsu: The business conglomerates that originated in the early Meiji period, when state industries were sold off to private companies. Privately owned companies, such as Mitsui and Mitsubishi, branched out, with government help, into many different enterprises, including banks, mines, heavy industry, and trading firms, which monopolized much of the Japanese economy. Although the owners of the family firms were dispossessed during the American occupation after World War II, the *zaibatsu* continued in a different, though not necessarily less monopolistic, form.

BIBLIOGRAPHY

If one were to read nothing else on the history of modern Japan, Marius Jansen's *The Making of Modern Japan* (Cambridge, Mass.: Harvard University Press, 2000) contains pretty much everything one needs to know. I owe a great debt to Professor Jansen's magisterial work. But there are other classics that cannot really be missed. *East Asia: The Modern Transformation* (Boston: Houghton Mifflin Co., 1960), by John K. Fairbank, Edwin O. Reischauer, and Albert M. Craig, is still a reference work I use all the time.

On the confrontation of Tokugawa Japan with the West, I benefited a great deal from Donald Keene's *The Japanese Discovery of Europe* (London: Routledge and Kegan Paul, 1952), especially for the discussion on Honda Toshiaki, the enlightened imperialist. A witty and well-documented account of Commodore Perry's arrival, and the political struggles this unleashed, is *Yankees in the Land of the Gods* (New York: Viking, 1990), by Peter Booth Wiley; the quotations from Perry's translator, the Reverend Samuel Wells Williams, are from this book. For the intellectual climate in late Tokugawa Japan, I turned to Masao Murayama's *Studies in the Intellectual History of Tokugawa Japan* (Princeton: Princeton University Press, 1974) and Grant K. Goodman's *Japan: The Dutch Experience* (London: Athlone, 1986). Another invaluable source, especially on the Mito School and its offshoots, is *Anti-Foreignism and Western Learning in Early-Modern Japan* (Cambridge, Mass.: Harvard University Press, 1986), by Bob Tadashi Wakabayashi. Much has been written about Sakamoto Ryoma, the swordsman turned constitutionalist. I used Marius Jansen's *Sakamoto Ryoma and the Meiji*

Restoration (Princeton: Princeton University Press, 1961). Those who wish to delve deeper into the intellectual life of this period might look at Marius Jansen's *China and the Tokugawa World* (Cambridge, Mass.: Harvard University Press, 1992).

To understand what it felt like for an educated Japanese to live in the Meiji period, it is probably best to read a few novels by Natsume Soseki, especially *Kokoro* (1914). This and other books of the time are discussed in Donald Keene's *Dawn to the West* (New York: Holt, Rinehart and Winston, 1984). Being rather close to the Meiji spirit himself, Keene is an invaluable guide and a superb translator. The translations of Takamura Kotaro's poems quoted in this book are his. My quotations from that other great Meiji figure, Fukuzawa Yukichi, are from *The Autobiography of Fukuzawa Yukichi* (New York: Columbia University Press, 1968), translated by Eiichi Kiyooka. A good book on the Meiji theater is J. Thomas Rimer's *Towards a Modern Japanese Theater: Kishida Kunio* (Princeton: Princeton University Press, 1974). For the early history of Japanese cinema, Donald Richie and Joseph L. Anderson's *The Japanese Film* (New York: Grove Press, 1959) is still the classic text. Julia Meech-Pekarik's *The World of the Meiji Print* (New York: Weatherhill, 1986) is about far more than woodcuts. It is full of wonderful descriptions. I lifted the passages by Pierre Loti about the goings-on at the Deer Park Pavilion from her book. Mishima Yukio's lament about Meiji prudery is from his introduction to a splendid book of photographs by Yato Tamotsu, now scandalously out of print, entitled *Naked Festival* (New York: Weatherhill, 1968).

On the ideology of modern nationalism, I can think of no better or more engaging book than Carol Gluck's *Japan's Modern Myths: Ideology in the Late Meiji Period* (Princeton: Princeton University Press, 1985). I would not know what to do without it. On Japanese empire building, I find *The Japanese Colonial Empire, 1895–1945* (Princeton: Princeton University Press, 1984), edited by Ramon Myers and Mark Peattie, indispensable. Roger W. Bowen's *Rebellion and Democracy in Meiji Japan* (Berkeley: University of California Press, 1980) was of great use to me for the People's Rights Movement and other revolts against authority.

Edward Seidensticker's *Low City, High City* (New York: Knopf, 1983) offers evocative, elegiac descriptions of Taisho-period Tokyo. This should be read together with some of his translations of that great nostalgist Nagai Kafu. If nothing else, one should read *A Strange Tale from East of the River*. Less enjoyable, but for some perhaps equally fascinating, are the writings of Kita Ikki. I took my quotations from *Kita Ikki Ron* (Tokyo: Gendai Hyoronsha, 1981), by Matsumoto Kenichi, but the standard work on Kita in English is George M. Wilson's *Radical Nationalist in Japan: Kita Ikki, 1883–1937* (Cambridge, Mass.: Harvard University Press, 1969). Just as interesting, though obviously a book of its time, is D. C. Holtom's *Modern Japan and Shinto Nationalism* (Chicago: University of Chicago Press, 1943). An important source for the 1936 revolt is Ben-Ami Shillony's *Revolt in Japan: The Young Officers and the February 26, 1936 Incident* (Princeton: Princeton University Press, 1973). On the modern history of the imperial house, and particularly Hirohito's education, I found *Hirohito and the Making of Modern Japan* (New York: HarperCollins, 2000), by Herbert P. Bix, of enormous benefit.

Manchuria is becoming a hot topic now, but no one writing on this subject can afford to ignore *Japan's Total Empire* (Berkeley: University of California Press, 1998), by Louise Young. I used it extensively, especially for its information on popular culture and government propaganda. The Nanjing massacre is perhaps an even more fashionable topic. Almost everything written about it has a political bias. For a decent liberal/left Japanese view, one should read Honda Katsuichi's *The Nanjing Massacre* (New York: M. E. Sharpe, 1999). My quotation of the Japanese soldier who fought in Nanjing is from *The Other Nuremberg,* by Arnold C. Brackman (London: Collins, 1989), an excellent account of the Tokyo War Crimes Tribunal. The battle of Nomonhan is exhaustively described in Alvin D. Cox's *Nomonhan: Japan Against Russia, 1939* (Stanford: Stanford University Press, 1985).

One of the best and best-known accounts of the attack on Pearl Harbor is by Gordon Prange, entitled *At Dawn We Slept: The Untold Story of Pearl Harbor* (New York: McGraw-Hill, 1981). On the diplomacy that preceded the attack, I used *Toward Pearl Harbor: The Diplomatic Exchange Between Japan and the United States, 1899–1941* (Princeton: Princeton University Press, 1991), edited by Ralph E. Shaffer. Hayashi Fusao, in *Daitoa Senso Koteiron* (Tokyo: Yamato Bunko, 1978), quotes some Japanese reactions. I cite the literary critic Okuna Takao. One can disagree, as I do, with some of its premises, but as a history of wartime mentalities, John W. Dower's *War Without Mercy: Race and Power in the Pacific War* (New York: Pantheon, 1986) is a mine of information. A much slimmer but equally thought-provoking essay related to this subject is *An Intellectual History of Wartime Japan, 1931–1945* (London: Kegan Paul International, 1986), by Tsurumi Shunsuke. I also find myself reaching again and again for Akira Irye's *Power and Culture: The Japanese-American War 1941–1945* (Cambridge, Mass.: Harvard University Press, 1981). Japan's surrender is well documented in Robert J. Butow, *Japan's Decision to Surrender* (Stanford: Stanford University Press, 1954). For an overall picture of the war, allowing for a left/liberal bias, Ienaga Saburo's *The Pacific War 1931–1945* (New York: Pantheon, 1978) is still useful.

The best, most exhaustive, and in my view fairest study of Japan under Allied occupation is John Dower's *Embracing Defeat: Japan in the Aftermath of World War II* (New York: W. W. Norton, 1999). For the insider's view, one can turn with profit to *Remaking Japan: The American Occupation as New Deal* (New

York: Free Press, 1987), by Theodore Cohen, edited by Herbert Passin. A highly original take on occupation cultural policies is *Mr. Smith Goes to Tokyo: Japanese Cinema Under the American Occupation, 1945–1952* (Washington, D.C.: Smithsonian, 1992), by Kyoko Hirano. Apart from Arnold C. Brackman's book, which I already mentioned, Richard H. Minear's *Victor's Justice: The Tokyo War Crimes Trial* (Princeton: Princeton University Press, 1971) cannot be left out of any study of the Tokyo trials. Its sharp point of view is only one of the book's virtues. I also benefited from the intensive scholarship of Meirion and Susie Harries in their *Sheathing the Sword: The Demilitarization of Japan* (London: Hamilton, 1987).

Dan Kurzman's *Kishi and Japan: The Search for the Sun* (New York: Astor-Honor, 1960) gives the old rogue too much credit but was useful to me nonetheless. Life in the ruins of Tokyo, and the consequent rebirth of the city, is beautifully evoked in Edward Seidensticker's *Tokyo Rising: The City Since the Great Earthquake* (New York: Knopf, 1990). Oshima Nagisa's diary entry is from a collection of his essays, *Taikenteki Sengo Eizoron* (Tokyo: Asahi Shimbunsha, 1975). For a discussion, from a conservative point of view, of the postwar constitution, I recommend (and quoted from) Kataoka Tetsuya's *The Price of a Constitution: The Origin of Japan's Postwar Politics* (New York: Crane Russak, 1991). Chalmers Johnson's *MITI and the Japanese Miracle* (Stanford: Stanford University Press, 1982) is good on the postwar economy. And for documentation I was helped greatly by *Japan: A Documentary History* (New York: M. E. Sharpe, 1997), by David J. Lu.

There is much, much more, of course. Great and scholarly works have been left out of this summary list, but I have confined myself to the books that were of particular use to me in writing my short history. I can only hope this has the effect of an hors d'oeuvre, which might whet the appetite for richer courses to come.

INDEX

ABOUT THE AUTHOR

IAN BURUMA studied and worked in Japan for many years. He is the author of *Bad Elements, The Missionary and the Libertine, Anglomania, A Japanese Mirror, God's Dust, The Wages of Guilt,* and *Playing the Game.* He lives in London.

A NOTE ON THE TYPE

The principal text of this Modern Library edition
was set in a digitized version of Janson, a typeface that
dates from about 1690 and was cut by Nicholas Kis,
a Hungarian working in Amsterdam. The original matrices have
survived and are held by the Stempel foundry in Germany.
Hermann Zapf redesigned some of the weights and sizes for
Stempel, basing his revisions on the original design.